PERGAMON GENERAL PSYCHOLOGY SERIES

Editors: Arnold P. Goldstein, *Syracuse University*
Leonard Krasner, *SUNY, Stony Brook*

THE PSYCHIATRIC PROGRAMMING OF PEOPLE:

Neo-Behavioral Orthomolecular Psychiatry

PGPS-25

THE PSYCHIATRIC PROGRAMMING OF PEOPLE:

Neo-Behavioral Orthomolecular Psychiatry

H. L. Newbold, M.D.

Department of Psychiatry
Lenox Hill Hospital
New York

PERGAMON PRESS INC.

New York . Toronto . Oxford . Sydney . Braunschweig

PERGAMON PRESS INC.
Maxwell House, Fairview Park, Elmsford, N.Y. 10523

PERGAMON OF CANADA, LTD.
207 Queen's Quay West, Toronto 117, Ontario

PERGAMON PRESS LTD.
Headington Hill Hall, Oxford

PERGAMON PRESS (AUST.) PTY. LTD.
19 Boundary Street, Rushcutters Bay, Sydney, N.S.W.

VIEWEG & SOHN GmbH
Burgplatz 1, Braunschweig

Printed in the United States of America
08 016791 8

For:

Son-Oak Rhee
    and
A. Hoffer, M.D., Ph.D.
Humphry Osmond, M.R.C.S., D.P.M.
Linus Pauling, Ph.D.
William H. Philpott, M.D.
B. F. Skinner, Ph.D.
John W. Tintera, M.D.

Contents

Preface

This work is an attempt to integrate the behavioral aspects of life with the biochemical base upon which all living creatures exist. As a means of building my thesis, I used the cybernetic model of the computer.

This material constitutes a philosophical approach to all problems of behavior, an overall theory to understand both normal and abnormal behavior.

Anyone who treats emotional illness soon finds himself floating through space unless he has a firm overview of just what he is attempting to accomplish, of how he will go about curing the patient, and of the goals which he may achieve with a particular patient. This is not a "how-to" book, but rather is an orientation encompassing all forms of treatment, from electro-shock therapy to psychoanalysis, binding them all into a single theory, into a unified whole.

Hopefully, any intelligent person who seeks a deep understanding of himself and of those accompanying him on his journey through time will feel a smile float across his face as he develops new insights while reading this volume.

Any work which is original will raise clouds of controversy because it offends some established authorities and disturbs the peace of mind of all who are forced to reconsider those theories which they cherish as the beams that support their philosophies.

The professor of medicine who spent forty years learning how to thump a chest, listen to the vibrations brought forth with his hands, and interpret these signals did not receive the advent of the X-ray machine with much grace. The device stripped him of his most valuable possession: knowledge. Suddenly any first-year medical student could take an X-ray picture of a chest and know more about the diseases of the heart and lungs than the professor could discover with his hands and ears in a lifetime.

The idea of attacking social ills with biological tools, though not new, still comes as a shock to most readers. The truth is the social sciences have yet to accept the nineteenth century's most startling discovery: Darwin's observations on evolution. But this approach is beginning to be accepted more as the years go by. Recently a major popular, and rather conservative, national magazine devoted its cover picture and lead story to genetic engineering. It is to be hoped that such honest journalism will help roll back the prejudice which still pervades the area of genetic engineering, and that the social sciences will at last be eased into the nineteenth century if not yet the twentieth.

A word about my dedication. The first name mentioned was, of course, placed there for personal reasons: dedicated to one who has enriched my life. Most of the others were included because of the significant work they have done, either theoretical or practical, in the field of schizophrenia, a disorder in which I am especially interested. Even if the orthomolecular approach to serious emotional illnesses should someday prove to be unfruitful, which I strongly doubt, these men will have given a new dignity to the person suffering from schizophrenia and will have helped bring this major illness back into the fold of the medical profession where it belongs as much as diabetes or hypertension.

Lastly, I have used the term orthomolecular to include substances normally present in the body, as well as chemicals foreign to the body. Vitamin E, for example, alters the permeability of the cell membrane toward normality (orthomolecularity), but so may diphenylhydantoin sodium (Dilantin). Since it seems very unlikely at this point that all enzyme system defects will someday be corrected by the use of substances normally present in the body, and as, in the practical everyday treatment of schizophrenia, many foreign chemicals are employed even by those psychiatrists who term themselves orthomolecular psychiatrists, and since these foreign chemicals do have the net effect of normalizing (orthomolecularizing) the neurone, it seems reasonable to include every psychoactive chemical which acts to normalize the nerve cells in the term orthomolecular.

In closing, I would like to thank those men mentioned in the dedication for what they have taught me, for widening my horizons, and making my life infinitely more interesting.

Private Practice, New York   H. L. NEWBOLD, M.D.
Formerly Instructor in Neurology and
* Psychiatry, Northwestern University,*
* School of Medicine, Chicago*

PART I

The Basic Structure of Man

CHAPTER 1

Introduction

Quite simply, the premise of this book is to establish a theory of personality and therapy based upon laboratory evidence from: (1) instrumental behavioral learning, (2) psychochemistry*, and (3) the computer.

Many persons are familiar with the Skinner box, but since it is so important in the understanding of the material to follow, a brief description is given.

A Skinner box is a container with a bar at one end. The bar is so rigged that when pressed, a pellet of food falls into a dish. When a hungry rat is placed in this box, it makes random explorations. Sooner or later, it presses the bar, at which time a pellet of food falls into the feeding dish. After eating the pellet of food, the rat again makes random explorations, but eventually presses the bar again and is rewarded with another pellet of food. The second press occurs sooner than the first, because the rat has begun to learn (is being programmed) that pressure on the bar earns him the desired food. Soon the rat, whenever it is hungry, goes directly to the bar, presses it and receives the desired food.

Skinner would say that reinforcement of the rat's behavior (bar pressing) with food has brought about conditioned behavior. To be more specific, this experiment constitutes an example of instrumental conditioning, since the reward is contingent upon a certain instrumental behavior (bar pressing).

The author chooses to look upon the central nervous system of the rat as a computer, a device to receive information, integrate information with previously stored information, and to give an appropriate response based upon a Master Plan. The act of learning to press the bar for food constitutes a programming of this rat's computer. The computer is presented with a Master Plan: to eat. The rat's computer is programmed to solve this problem by initiating a behavioral pattern, i.e., pressing the bar.

---

* Psychochemistry includes not only chemicals which act upon the neuron, but also allergies which change the neuron, electro convulsive therapy, narco electro therapy, carbon dioxide therapy, etc.

It should be clearly understood in the beginning that a computer is made of two basic parts—hardware and software. The hardware consists of the basic mechanical construction of the computer: copper wiring, vacuum tubes, magnetic tapes, etc., depending upon the particular type of computer. The software is the information programmed into the computer. For example, a computer may be programmed with the information that $2 + 2 = 4$. If this were all the computer were programmed for, then $2 + 2 = 4$ would constitute the entire software of the computer.

In the case of the rat, it is clear that its central nervous system (computer) is also divided into hardware and software. Thus if the hardware of the central nervous system (CNS) is disturbed either physically or chemically, it will (like a broken computer) not function properly. That is to say that the damaged computer (brain) cannot be programmed properly and will not effectively solve Master Plans (problems). If the central nervous system (CNS) is damaged by cutting away certain parts of the brain, the rat's hardware will be damaged and will not function properly. If, on the other hand, the CNS is damaged chemically, for example by an injection of insulin, again the hardware of the computer (CNS) will be damaged (non-ortho-molecular) and thus will not function properly.

The rat's computer can also malfunction because of damage to the software of its computer (CNS) by programming it incorrectly. For example, if the rat received an electric shock (rather than a pellet of food) the second time he pressed the bar for food, this would confuse him and interfere with his being programmed to press the bar to solve his hunger problem. Now we may move directly to experimental observations on people.

A disturbed fifteen-year-old girl was sent to a hospital because she was incorrigible in her home setting. She had run away, stayed the night with various men, refused to attend school, and physically attacked her parents.

When she arrived at the hospital she was angry to the point of being uncontrollable. For this reason she was placed in isolation, a bare room. This room constituted a part of her Skinner box. She was told that she could earn a black poker chip by washing dishes. She would be given an opportunity to wash dishes for one hour three times a day. For each hour of dish washing, she would earn a black poker chip. She could exchange each black poker chip for a meal. Whether or not she chose to wash dishes was entirely up to her. No force was to be used. The subject sat in the corner for the rest of the day. But she was a rather buxom girl who had obviously enjoyed eating in the past. As expected, the next morning she requested to wash dishes. She was completely cooperative when taken to the kitchen. Afterwards she was given a black poker chip. This she exchanged for a meal.

After faithfully following this procedure for several days, she asked how she might leave the confinement of her room and was told that if she washed dishes for an extra hour each day she could earn a red poker chip. With three red poker chips she would be able to buy her way out of isolation and be allowed to live in the dormitory and take part in the normal activities of the hospital. She cheerfully earned her red poker chips and thus was able to buy her way into the larger Skinner box, i.e., the regular hospital program.

We might say that this girl's computer had been programmed to release her energies in a socially approved activity—dish washing. Getting the dirty dishes washed was not the goal of the programming. The goal was to program this girl to discharge her energies in socially acceptable channels, to rehabilitate her.

Though not strictly true, this fifteen-year-old girl should be, for present purposes, considered an example of an improperly programmed computer— a computer with damaged software. (Later in the volume it is pointed out that subjects such as this may have damaged hardware, also, but her damage is here considered software damage.)

Now change the subject living inside the Skinner box. Replace her with a man hallucinating from LSD. Now he is withdrawn into a corner brushing at the imaginary red hot oil from Mars that he thinks is being poured on him.

"Water," he muttered. "You want water?" He nodded his head. He was told that he might wash dishes for half an hour. For this activity he would be given a black poker chip. He could exchange this black poker chip for three glasses of water. He needed only to say when he was ready to earn the chip.

The man only stared for a moment then retreated into his hallucination. He was asked again if he would like a drink of water. He nodded his head. The instructions were repeated, but he did not bother to listen. He continued to brush at the imaginary steaming oil.

With the girl, behavior therapy succeeded because she had a relatively normal hardware computer which could be programmed. With the man who suffered from hallucinations, behavior therapy failed because the hardware of his computer was chemically damaged and could not be programmed in the usual manner.

The male patient was started on megavitamin injections of niacin and ascorbic acid, as well as conventional doses of Multiple B complex vitamins. Also he was given water, glucose and saline by veniclysis. Thus the major immediate damage in the hardware of his computer was chemically repaired. This is an example of orthomolecular psychiatry, i.e., the molecules (chemistry) of his brain were normalized by the use of chemical compounds.

Linus Pauling (1968) would agree that this patient's treatment was ortho-molecularly oriented since the physician supplied substances normally present in the body, but, presumably, in inadequate concentrations in this sick man's body.

Had a major tranquilizer been used the author would consider it also an example of orthomolecular psychiatry. This particular point is taken up later when the neural synapse is discussed.

The next morning the patient was much better organized. He was still somewhat shaky, but the hot oil had disappeared and he was well in touch with his surroundings. When asked if he wanted breakfast, he stated that he was very hungry and would like wheat cakes. He was then told that he could wash dishes for an hour, earn a black poker chip which he might trade for breakfast. The patient eagerly requested to wash dishes. He washed the dishes, earned the poker chip and bought his breakfast with it.

Now this normalized (repaired hardware) computer was being program-med in the usual manner through behavioral techniques.

Conclusions

1. A computer with intact hardware can be programmed with the aid of routine behavioral techniques.

2. A computer with damaged hardware cannot be programmed through the use of routine behavioral techniques. It is understood that programming of a damaged hardware computer depends upon the relative amount of the damage and the strength of the stimulation. For example, if the room had been set on fire, the hallucinating patient might have shown a programming response.

3. Some abnormal computers can be normalized (repaired) chemically and can then be programmed through the use of routine behavioral techniques.

The theoretical and practical aspects of these concepts constitute the remainder of this volume.

CHAPTER 2

Machine

Man = machine. Man is a machine. One definition of a machine is an apparatus for applying mechanical power. Thus a pair of pliers meets this definition of a machine. Pliers may be used to apply mechanical power; for example, to bend a piece of wire or tighten a bolt or pull a nail.

Clearly man too is a machine since he can use his heel to pry loose a stake, or use his hand to pluck an apple, or use his arm to lift a log.

CHAPTER 3

Energy

Man = machine + energy. Man is an energized machine. A pair of pliers is an example of a machine without energy; however, an automobile is an example of a machine which contains energy, power. Of itself (once set in motion) it can apply mechanical power.

One need only stand at the foot of a table and deliver a baby to know that man is born with a source of energy. The newborn baby pulls its arms against its chest, flexes its legs, opens its mouth, takes in a breath of air, and gives a cry.

Here we see a machine (legs, etc.) which discharges energy. The energy is contained in the machine.

CHAPTER 4

Computer

Man = machine + energy + computer. Man is an energized machine with a computer, a device to receive, store and integrate information and send out a response.

Many machines have been built with a servo type computer. An automobile (an energized machine) can be equipped with a speed regulator. When the dial of this speed regulator is set (programmed) at 60 miles an hour, the regulator remembers to make the automobile travel at the rate of 60 miles an hour. When the regulator receives information that the car's speed is slowing, it "remembers" that the car is to travel at a steady 60 miles an hour. It then feeds out information which makes the car accelerate up to 60 miles an hour. The automatic speed regulator has been programmed to seek homeostatasis, i.e., a 60 mile an hour speed.

Of course much more complicated computers have been constructed. These are discussed later in terms of more complex human functions.

Naturally the computer in man is the brain.

CHAPTER 5

Communicator

Man = machine + energy + computer + communicator. Man is an energized machine with a computer which uses a communicator to receive and send information.

We return again to the automobile with an automatic speed regulator. Here we find an energized machine with a computer which receives, integrates and gives out information through a communicator. A cable (communicator) extends from the drive shaft to a counterweighted governor which in turn uses an electrical impulse through a wire to communicate information to the throttle control.

Man's computer (brain) receives and sends information through its communicators (neurons).

CHAPTER 6

Biologically Programmed Computer

Man = machine + energy + communicator + Biologically Programmed Computer.

Man is an energized machine with a computer which uses a communicator to receive and send information. He is born with a Biologically Programmed Computer.

The speed regulator on the automobile comes from the factory set at a particular speed. Thus the speed regulator (computer) comes to the owner preprogrammed.

In the past, man's Biologically Programmed Computer (the preprogrammed part of his computer) has been referred to as his reflexes, drives, instincts, or inborn behavior patterns.

For example, the newborn baby is born biologically programmed for respiration. The respiration center in the brain (computer) is excited by a raising of the CO_2 level in the tissue, the respiratory center (computer) sends a message through the nerves (communicators) to the muscles (machine) of the chest, diaphragm, and face which expand the chest walls, lowers the diaphragm, creates a vacuum and opens the mouth. Air flows into the lungs to fill the vacuum.

All of this activity is brought about by the Biologically Programmed Computer which receives information, integrates it with other information and, through the communicators, initiates a particular response in the form of mechanical action designed to solve a Master Plan, i.e., maintain a biologically suitable oxygen tension in the tissues.

Of course newborn babies are born biologically programmed in many other ways. For example, the newborn baby is born biologically programmed to cry in response to discomfort, to close a fist about an object placed in the hand, etc. Much of the biological programming of the newborn's computer is apparent at birth. Other evidence of biological programming does not show itself until maturity.

For example, a newborn beagle puppy's computer has been born biologically programmed to give tongue while hunting and to follow prey primarily by the use of scent. It has not yet developed other capacities which are needed for hunting, thus we do not see evidence of this biological programming. However, we know it is present, or at least the genetic pattern is present that develops the Biologically Programmed Computer part of its nervous system so this behavior occurs as the puppy's computer matures.

In the case of an Irish wolfhound, we have a newborn puppy with a computer biologically programmed to hunt silently and primarily by the use of sight. Adult Irish wolfhounds are silent while hunting and follow their prey visually.

These contrasting characteristic behavioral patterns are biologically programmed and are not learned from adult dogs.

CHAPTER 7

Homeostasis

Man = machine + energy + communicator + Biologically Programmed Computer + homeostasis.

Man is an energized machine with a Biologically Programmed Computer which uses a communicator to receive and send information. He seeks homeostasis.

Physically, chemically, socially, and psychologically man attempts to maintain homeostasis. His energy is discharged through behavioral patterns for homeostasis, otherwise he would die.

We see many homeostatic machines. The automatic speed control on the automobile is a computer designed to maintain homeostasis insofar as the speed of the car is concerned. When the speed increases, the mechanism shuts off the gasoline. The gasoline remains shut off until the car speed falls to a certain figure, at which time the accelerator is stimulated to feed more gasoline into the engine and increase the speed of the car until it reaches the predetermined figure.

The human machine must often maintain itself in a hostile physical environment. When the temperature in a room falls below the comfort level, the man moves into a different room, dons additional clothing or places another log on the fire. He attempts to maintain homeostasis, a body temperature of 98.7 degrees. If this approximate temperature is not maintained, he will die.

To maintain a suitable level of blood glucose, a man must eat. When the blood sugar level falls to a certain level, he is motivated to eat in order to maintain homeostasis. If he does not eat he will die.

Man must also maintain psychological homeostasis. If a man is deprived of all contact with his fellow men, and deprived of all sensory stimulation, he will become psychotic. The U.S. Navy has regularly been able to produce

17

hallucinations and disorganized behavior by encasing a man in a steel ball and lowering him into a shaft of water for a number of hours, where the subject will live in complete darkness, complete silence, complete sensory deprivation except for the monotonous touch of the smooth steel shell which encloses him. Thus man seeks stimulation from other people and from his environment to maintain homeostasis, to prevent an emotional collapse.

A juvenile delinquent may become so enraged with his father that he runs away from home to escape either: a psychotic break—insanity, complete disorganization of the mind, or from killing his father. By choosing to run away he places his existence in a position more favorable than the one he would have occupied should he have had a psychotic break or killed his father. The act of running away from home is motivated by a desire to maintain homeostasis.

A woman is married to an impotent man. Because of mounting sexual needs (which she may feel leads to such a lack of homeostasis that a psychotic break is imminent) she has an affair. She is trying to maintain homeostasis. But this attempt fails because she becomes so guilt ridden that she feels she will disintegrate, become psychotic. She visits a psychologist and tells him about her unacceptable act and her unbearable guilt. He accepts her as a worthwhile person in spite of her mistake. She thus alters her Self-Conception and tends to reach homeostasis. He then tries to help her learn to handle her sexual needs by discharging them in socially acceptable ways (sublimation) and to reach a more lasting homeostasis. If her sexual needs are so great she cannot release them in secondary ways, he may approve of her masturbatory acts and thus help her reach homeostasis by changing her Self-Conception (reprogramming her) so that she believes a woman may still be a worthwhile person in spite of masturbation. Other programming is of course possible: a divorce or even, if no other course seems possible, a well-regulated extra-marital relationship. Thus she reaches homeostasis. The psychologist may refer her to a psychiatrist who places her on a tranquilizer which reduces the disorganizing anxiety brought about by sexual tension and thus she may reach homeostasis.

A man may feel discomfort because he conceives of himself as being inferior. He may work sixteen hours a day constructing a housing project and buy an expensive automobile in an attempt to feel superior. He is motivated by a desire for homoeostasis.

CHAPTER 8

Compartmentalized Computer

Man = machine + energy + communicator + homeostasis + compartmentalized computer.

Man is an energized machine which seeks homeostasis through communicators which receive and send information to and from his computer.

It has already been mentioned that a computer is a device that can receive, store, integrate, and send information to aid in homeostasis. One part of man's computer is singled out: his Biologically Programmed Computer.

The entire computer of man is divided into three compartments:

1. The Biologically Programmed Computer (BPC).
2. The Socially Programmed Computer (SPC), which includes Self-Conception.
3. The TOTE (Test-Operate Test-Exit) Computer (TOTEC) which includes Master and Minor Plans, testing, accepting or rejecting, and integration of the programs of the Biologically Programmed Computer and the Socially Programmed Computer in order that man may act on his environment to achieve homeostasis.

The Biologically Programmed Computer (BPC) has been mentioned and defined as consisting of inherited programs. The Socially Programmed Computer (SPC) is that part of man's computer which has been programmed through social contacts and is dealt with later in more detail. A TOTE (Test-Operate Test-Exit) Computer is the most complex of the three computers.

Since an understanding of the conception of the TOTE computer is of importance for the psychological understanding and treatment of man, it is dealt with in this chapter.

A computer can be programmed for problem solving, i.e., given a Master Plan. Much of man's computer (brain) is engaged in problem solving since this is necessary in the search for homeostasis. It can be programmed to solve problems by either an *alogorithmic* approach or by a *heuristic* approach.

If programmed to take the *alogorithmic* problem solving approach, the computer would consider all the possibilities or combinations of possible facts to solve the problem. Obviously this is an inefficient computer. Before the human computer would come up with much useful information with *alogorithmic* problem solving techniques, the owner might well find himself in difficulties. Thus, if a primitive man used this form of problem solving to locate his favorite hunting ground he might starve before finding any game.

If the computer is programmed for *heuristic* problem solving, then we have a much more efficient instrument which can program itself (learn from experience) as well as pursue or reject promising paths toward problem solving. For example, it may be programmed for checker playing. The (Master Plan) problem: win a game of checkers. The computer is then programmed with all the rules of the game. Furthermore, it is programmed to pursue promising channels of play and to reject unpromising channels of play. It can even be programmed to program (teach and remember) itself so that it will not make the same mistake a second time. Thus we have a TOTE (Test-Operate Text-Exit) computer, a computer which works like man (the brain) in that it learns (is programmed) through trial and error.

Such a programmed computer plays a good game of checkers the first time, but each game of checkers it plays improves. Theoretically, a large enough heuristic programmed (TOTE) computer can be built so that eventually it will always play a perfect game of checkers and beat any human pitted against it. The similarities to human thinking are obvious.

A computer which can be programmed for solving the problems of a Master Plan, can test and reject directions of effort, and can reprogram itself to eliminate mistakes in the future, is called a TOTE computer. It uses heuristic problem solving techniques.

Now that we have identified the TOTE computer, we may proceed in the next three chapters to discuss the compartmentalized computer (brain) of man.

CHAPTER 9

An Analysis of
The Biologically Programmed
Computer

In Chapter 5 the Biologically Programmed Computer was discussed briefly; however, now that other essential concepts have been introduced, it is worthwhile to discuss the Biologically Programmed Computer at further length.

The Biologically Programmed Computer (BPC) includes those parts of the computer system which are passed on to the individual through inheritance. They are either present at birth, or develop automatically as the computer (brain) grows to maturity. The BPC (Biologically Programmed Computer) can be and is modified by the TOTEC (Test-Operate Test-Exit Computer). The essential quality of the BPC (Biologically Programmed Computer) however, remains unchanged.

The BPC is subdivided into three sections: Reflex Programs, Behavioral Programs, and Expanding Programs.

Reflex Programs

Reflex Programs are certainly present at birth in the BPC. We have given the example of breathing. When the carbon dioxide content of the body builds up to a given point, the reflex of breathing is fully initiated and continues to function throughout the life of the organism. The communicator (nerve) from the brain stem (computer) sends a message to the muscles of the chest and diaphragm so that the chest expands, creates a vacuum and thus air flows into the lungs.

Other evidences of the Reflex Programs within the BPC at birth: the moro reflex, tonic neck reflex, sucking reflex, grasping reflex, plantar reflex, and others.

Behavioral Programs

Behavioral Programs are present in the BPC. The study of this aspect of human behavior has been greatly neglected, but this area of research offers great promise for the future.

Skinner, in *Science and Human Behavior*, put his finger on the biological foundations of behavior when he stated: "Behavior is as much a part of the organism as are its anatomical features." This rule is universal whether it be a pine tree, a sea turtle, a dog, or a man.

We have already cited the beagle dog as an example of complex behavior resulting from the Behavioral Programs within the Biologically Programmed Computer (BPC). The beagle gives tongue while hunting its prey and hunts primarily by scent.

A great deal of work has been done on the genetic aspects of behavior at the Jackson Memorial Laboratory where Ginsburg, Scott and others have effectively developed strains of German Shepherd guide dogs for the blind. The laboratory had set a goal of fifty guide dogs a year, but during the first five years of work was only able to turn out, as a maximum, nine dogs a year. This represented an 8% success. However, in recent years this figure has risen to 95%. The improvement was accomplished almost entirely through selective breeding for desired behavioral characteristics. Some of the characteristics which were successfully *bred out* included:

1. Mental dullness.
2. Excessive ear sensitivity.
3. Excessive body sensitivity.
4. Dull body sensitivity.
5. Dull ear sensitivity.
6. Fawning personality.
7. Fear.
8. Lack of awareness of moving objects.
9. Biting.
10. Intractability.
11. Lack of stability, neurotic personality.

The quality of fawning personality, for example, is a complex programmed unit. All will agree that a dog which carries the inborn programming (BPC) of a fawning personality will have all his later development colored by this trait.

For practical purposes, when dealing with man, one aspect of the behavioral part of the Biologically Programmed Computer (BPC) is of pressing interest—tractability.

By definition, tractability refers to being easily managed, docile, compliant, governable. We are all aware that mules are less tractable than race horses. If an animal is tractable, it can easily be programmed through behavioral techniques. If an animal is intractable, it is less easily programmed.

Good examples of inherited (Biologically Programmed Computers) tractability and intractability have come from the Jackson Memorial Laboratory. To be a good guide dog, a dog must be relatively tractable, must have the personality makeup (Biologically Programmed Computer) which allows him to be rather easily programmed for guiding the blind.

Through controlled breeding, the group at Jackson Memorial Laboratory has greatly increased the percentage of guide dogs which are bred to meet their standards of tractability. Clearly, tractability is an inherited characteristic in dogs. A striking example is their work with besinji and cocker spaniel dogs. Besinjis are well known for being intractable, for having a mind of their own and for being rather independent of the owners. Cocker spaniels, on the other hand, tend to be easy-going dogs who are warm and friendly, tractable, and thus good subjects for social programming. It was discovered that the besinjis required something like twice as many leash jerks to leash train them, compared to the number of jerks required to leash train cocker spaniels. Thus we find an inherited trait (tractability) which greatly facilitates programming.

We might conclude that some types of Biologically Programmed Computers are more suitable for behavior therapy, the reprogramming of the Socially Programmed Computer.

Tractability has a profound effect upon the programming of the human computer, i.e., child rearing and behavioral psychotherapy. For example, a tractable child is easily toilet trained without the stress developed in the toilet training (programming of the Socially Programmed Computer) of the intractable child. The intractable child develops an entirely different Self-Conception (Self-Conception becomes a part of the Socially Programmed Computer) from that of the tractable child.

Social pressures (programming) are exerted with much more force on the intractable child. "You're a bad boy," the mother repeatedly tells the intractable child because he does not easily obey her commands, does not conveniently lend himself to being programmed. In turn, the intractable child develops a hostile attitude toward his programmers (parents) which is later directed toward all authority figures and thus complicates his interaction with other people and with the general social structure in which he lives.

All forms of psychotherapy, because they depend, in part, upon acceptance of the patient by the therapist as a basically worthwhile person, modify the patient's Self-Conception. Thus the patient's Socially Programmed Computer is reprogrammed by the therapist to be less self-punitive. The patient's Self-Conception can be altered, and so his whole outlook toward his past programmers (parents) and authoritative figures is altered.

Psychochemicals greatly alter the trait of tractability (BPC) so that the patient becomes more tractable and thus reprogramming by the therapist is made easier. But this subject is dealt with at greater length later.

The human mother who has reared several children is well aware of great difference in the personalities of her children, differences which seem to exceed any difference in the way she has reared the children.

In an interesting longitudinal study of children from the time of birth, Fries and Woolf noted activity types. Marked differences were noted in the development of these children. Not only the world around them, but the mothers themselves treated the active and the passive child in different ways. It was noted that when the parents were normal, children tended to deviate toward the median. But the active children never became passive or the passive children active. When the parents were neurotic, the children tended to deviate away from the median. Thus the active child became more active and the passive child more passive.

The subject of behavioral genetics cannot be fully explored in a volume such as this. The reader who is interested in this enormously important aspect of human behavior is referred to Fuller and Thompson's *Behavior Genetics*.

A few of the well established behavioral patterns (programs) which are generally considered to be primarily hereditary (BPC) in composition include:

1. Tractability.
2. Ability to love (approach to or withdrawal from people).
3. General excitability.
4. Energy level.
5. General intelligence.
6. Special intelligence.
7. Shyness.
8. Verbalization.

9. Dominance.
10. Drug and food preference and susceptibility.
11. Motor skills.
12. Sexual drive.
13. Maleness or femaleness.
14. Laterality.
15. Sleep patterns.

Many other behavioral patterns could be included now. More will be added as knowledge is gained in this new field.

Expanding Programs

The third compartment of the Biologically Programmed Computer is made up of the Expanding Programs, which are close to what in the past has been referred to as aggressiveness (referring to the act of mastery and acquisition) and sexuality.

All living creatures are biologically programmed to expand, grow larger, take over more territory, kill, consume, crowd out the neighbors, and, if possible, take over the entire earth and universe. For example, a pine tree has been biologically programmed to expand. Its roots dig down deep into the soil and spread sideways. If the roots of fellow pine trees are in the vicinity, it competes with them for soil and water and attempts to get as much as possible for itself. Young sapling pine trees grow upward to reach more sunlight and, in so doing, may cut off the sun from other saplings. Some of the sapling pine trees die in the process of competition. The pine tree expands also by reproduction. It releases seed into the air, thus insuring that other pine trees grow. We might consider that each offspring pine tree represents an extension of the parent pine tree, thus the parent tree is actually expanding by reproducing pine trees like itself.

If competition were not present, then, at least theoretically, pine trees would take over the world. But, of course, the parent pine tree and the off-spring pine tree must compete with all other living things. An oak tree might overshadow the pine tree because of an environment more favorable to the expansion of oak trees than pine trees. Man rips roads through pine forests and lays concrete and thus limits the Expanding Program of pine trees, to give only two examples of competition.

Raymond Dart, of Johannesburg, published a paper in *The International Anthropological and Linguistic Review* in 1953, entitled "The Predatory

Transition from Ape to Man." This paper, and its popularization by Ardrey, has shaken the scientific world. Dart pointed out that man is descended from a group of killer, meat-eating primates. Man himself has killed to live, has been selectively bred (BPC) to construct more and more efficient weapons for killing for over a million years. The act of killing his opponents, as a part of his Expanding Program, has been biologically programmed into man over these many generations. Today, whenever any discussion of man arises, one fact must forever remain in the foreground if man is to be understood: *Man is a killer.*

If anyone doubts that killing programs still occupy an important place in man's Biologically Programmed Computer, let him read his daily paper or switch on his television set. In the paper we find short summaries of who has killed whom during the past twenty-four hours in the local community, in the state, in the nation, and overseas. Like ball game scores the newspaper publishes how many American and Vietnamese are killed each day in a very human game called war, where nations square off against one another like boys who fight on the playgrounds of the world for the sheer joy of fighting. On the TV set may be found cops and robbers, cowboys and Indians, spies and counterspies all engaged in the business of killing one another so the viewer can experience a vicarious outlet for the killing programs of his BPC.

Man, like all other living creatures, is biologically programmed to expand as much as possible. He is limited by both the environment and his fellow men in his biologically programmed tendency to expand. He can successfully realize his expansion programs only by expressing them through social institutions.

The whole point in behavioral psychochemotherapy (as in all forms of child rearing and therapy for the emotionally ill) is to direct the discharge of man's BPC programs through socially approved institutions. A man is allowed to expand as far as possible under the regulations which society places upon him. Because of man's expanding tendencies it is necessary to limit the rules (by establishing social institutions) through which he may expand. The fact that man's life span is limited to seventy odd years also tends to limit his personal expansion.

A Henry Ford has the particular qualities which allow him to expand a great deal in a particular environment. But anti-trust laws were passed in order to limit such expansion. At last death put an end to his expansion. History affords many examples of persons who have expanded to encompass a great deal. For example, Caesar, Napoleon and Hitler all had great abilities for expansion, but each of them was struck down by his fellow men, and thus his expansion was limited.

It is a well known fact that during the height of her power, Great Britain followed a policy of balance of power. Whenever a nation or group of nations became threateningly powerful, she sided against them, thus she tended to limit their Expanding Programs. Today the United States follows a similar foreign policy in regard to the other great world power, Soviet Russia. One of the reasons the United States finds so many nations opposing it, is because other nations recognize the United States' great power, and attempt to limit it.

A man may expand himself by finishing college, getting a job and working hard at it. All the while he is competing with other men at work he must maintain a friendly attitude and not openly admit his expanding desires, lest he make everyone uncomfortable. "I just like to do a job well," he will say, rather than: "I plan to get as much power as possible, to expand my domain and the reaches of my personality as far as I can. While getting ahead I'm going to do everything possible to pull you other men under."

People attend cocktail parties in part so they can renew social contacts and thus maintain their power (expansion programs) by making certain they ally themselves with others in a friendly manner. They mill about at the cocktail party making small talk while they consume alcohol (a psychochemical) which tends to suppress their expansion drives. When these expansion tendencies are well under control, they can be less competitive with the other persons at the party. A bridge party is a different situation. Here the expansion problems are handled more directly. The participants are allowed to compete with one another, to attempt to expand, through the use of a game. Thus people can reinforce social contacts without fear of openly trying to conquer one another.

The study of leadership is interesting in view of man's desire to expand. We are all familiar with the name dropper: "Guess who sat beside me on the plane to New York?" "I can't imagine." "Cary Grant!" Thus the man is able to expand, to get more power by letting it be known that he is associated with a prominent name, a man who has achieved considerable expansion. Followers gather around in order to share the leader's expansion (power), and thus increase their own Expanding Programs.

Leaf through a fashion magazine and you find pictures of sexually desirable young ladies in suggestive poses wearing a dress manufactured by X Company. The implication is that if the women readers will only buy this dress they will be able to expand. They will become more sexually attractive. Therefore, they will attract a man who will marry them and thus give them the added expansion which comes with having a mate. Without bothering to go through the rigors of a university education, the woman can marry an educated man and thus share in all the expansion he has attained and will attain in the future. Also this man will impregnate her, allow her to reproduce their kind, and thus again, like the pine tree, expand. Innumerable examples of the desire to expand will occur to the reader.

Expanding Programs of the Biologically Programmed Computer (BPC) are, of course, a source of great frustrations (anger), because these Expanding Programs are in competition with Expanding Programs of others. For example, every man in an office is competing with every other man for promotion, hence more prestige, more power, more sexual attractiveness. Expanding programs are also a source of anger because social living with other humans demands that Expanding Programs be expressed in socially approved ways through socially established institutions. If Expanding Programs were not focused through social institutions, then it would not be possible for man to live together in social groups, and man is socially programmed, during the long dependency of childhood, so that he cannot be happy living without other people.

Child rearing consists of programming the Socially Programmed Computer. Psychotherapy consists of reprogramming of the Socially Programmed Computer. Psychochemotherapy is used to normalize (orthomolecularize) the abnormal (damaged hardware or software) computer so it can be programmed properly or reprogrammed during psychotherapy.

CHAPTER 10

The Socially Programmed Computer

The infant is born with a Biologically Programmed Computer, but this is a relatively primitively programmed computer which controls only certain basic activities.

In the sea turtle, for a contrasting example, the Biologically Programmed Computer is adequate to sustain much of its life. This animal never develops a Socially Programmed Computer of a size comparable to man's. The female turtle lays her eggs in the warm sand, covers them and goes back out to sea. The newly hatched turtles must depend entirely upon their Biologically Programmed Computers because they never meet their mother. Their Biologically Programmed Computers direct them to dig out of the sand, waddle down to the sea and begin their lives as independent beings. In the insect world we find members of their society which are born and live all their lives directed almost entirely by their Biologically Programmed Computers. Bees make their hives and even communicate with one another entirely through the use of their Biologically Programmed Computers.

The human infant, however, is a very helpless creature even with its Biologically Programmed Computer. Without the aid of its mother, or a mother substitute, it would die. The great number of years of total dependency means that man, more than any other animal, lives by the directions of his Socially Programmed Computer. The helpless infant's Biologically Programmed Computer causes it to reach out for the mother, to seek her warmth, her milk, her attention. In a similar manner the helpless, hungry infant activates a behavior pattern in the mother which is governed by her Biologically Programmed Computer. Each mother and child reach out for one another and weld a social bond which is the most powerful social bond the child ever forms. The character of this relationship affects all other relationships the infant may have with other people. The infant, because of its helplessness and the resultant dependency, enters into a bond with the mother which is called love. Love is always a close symbiosis in which each person gives and takes from one another. Love is thus programmed into the Socially Programmed Computer. The infant wants warmth, attention and milk. The mother wants to give warmth, attention and milk. In following their respective behaviors (dictated by their Biologically Programmed Computers) each fulfills the other's need.

But the infant needs the mother more than the mother needs the infant. Without the mother, or mother substitute, the infant would die. Without the infant, the mother would go through a period of emotional turmoil, but she would not die. Because the infant depends absolutely upon the mother, it soon learns that her approval and good will is of the utmost importance. This realization places it in a position to be socially programmed by her.

"That's my good boy," she says in later months when he performs his excretory functions at the socially approved time and place. The mother's approval of the child is very important to him, so important that he surrenders his independence (pleasures of haphazard excitory activity) in exchange for her approval (love). Thus she programs his Socially Programmed Computer.

When he goes to school the teacher (substitute mother) continues to program his Socially Programmed Computer by the use of behavioral techniques. She approves of his first crude attempts at reading and writing and thus encourages him to persist in this activity and to be further programmed.

Later in life he continues to be programmed by each social contact he makes, having been programmed by years of dependency to require the presence and, therefore, the approval of his fellow men. For example, if he obtains employment in the gray flannel world of business, the disapproval of his fellow workers programs him to wear gray flannel suits rather than the kind of flashy sport coat he might wear should he be working as an automobile salesman.

The psychotherapist is nothing but another programmer.

As indicated previously, the Socially Programmed Computer includes Self-Conception. The child develops a Self-Conception during the course of his Social Programming. The quality of the child's Self-Conception has an important bearing upon his personality formation. "You're always trying to misbehave," the mother (programmer) may tell the child with strong Expanding Programs, a hundred thousand times during the course of his dependency relationship with her. Thus the child may develop a poor self-image, may have his Socially Programmed Computer programmed so that he is punitive towards himself. If he has unusually strong Expanding Programs (aggressiveness), he may well be a "bad" child in terms of his relationship with his mother, and later, society. He may constantly attempt to dominate her (to expand), or he may be intractable and constantly resist her attempts at programming him.

This negative, self-depreciating programming is the source of what psychoanalysts refer to as "problems of receiving." The child develops inhibitions and guilt feelings, since his Socially Programmed Computer is programmed to hold him in check through its disapproval of him because of his antisocial tendencies, his needs to expand (be aggressive). Every person develops negative, self-depreciating programs because each person is, to one degree or another, pitted against his fellow men as he attempts to fulfill the Expanding Programs of his Biologically Programmed Computer.

But people with strong Expanding Programs in the BPC (very aggressive) tend to develop stronger self-punitive programs in their Socially Programmed Computers. The therapist frequently sees a man with unusually strong Expanding Programs sitting across the desk from him, a man who is clever and apparently would be a very able person if the Self-Conception part of his Socially Programmed Computer had not been programmed to defeat him. Rather than a successful man, the therapist finds a man mired down in a swamp of depression which is, in part, caused by his punitively programmed Socially Programmed Computer.

Society paralyzes these excessively expanding people in an attempt to hold them in check, otherwise the world would be filled with Caesars and Napoleons and Hitlers who would forever be leading mankind down a path of destruction. In later life, society destroys these Caesars, these Napoleons, these Hitlers, unless they have been held in check, and thus partially destroyed by their self-punitively programmed Self-Conception part of their Socially Programmed Computers. In one way or another, society places its needs before the needs of the individual, and destroys him unless he allows himself to be socially programmed to conform to society's needs.

Whenever possible in the course of child rearing (programming) a self-accepting Socially Programmed Computer should be developed. The child with strong Expanding Programs, for example, should be encouraged (programmed) to indulge in heavy, competitive sports where his expanding tendencies will be an asset rather than a liability. If a child with strong physical Expanding Programs were made to sit at a piano all afternoon and boringly practice musical scales, he would not have an opportunity to capitalize (be rewarded, find acceptable ways to expand) on his particular type of Expanding Programs. "You're a bad boy. You always want to go out and play instead of practicing your scales," the mother says, thus programming his Socially Programmed Computer (SPC) for punitive action against the boy. The boy grows up with a poor Self-Conception.

Another maneuver which is very successful in rearing the child with excessively strong Expanding Programs is to place him on a tranquilizer which reduces the force of his Expanding Programs and thus allows him to more easily fit into the social norms and develop a less self-punitive Socially Programmed Computer. The child therapist helps the mother select appropriate programming for her particular child. Thus the therapist might suggest that the child be allowed to give up music and join a baseball team. If the child is still too expanding, he should be placed on a tranquilizer. Once on the tranquilizer the child usually falls into the normal programming which is set up for the average child in school and in the home. When the child begins achieving in these areas, his Socially Programmed Computer begins to be reprogrammed by the rewards he receives for his achievements and thus his Self-Conception is altered toward a more accepting state. Many other examples of this mechanism will come immediately to the mind of the experienced therapist.

With older patients, the therapist himself becomes the parent, the programmer, who gives or withholds the reward of approval (behavior therapy) from the patient and thus aids not only in reprogramming the self-punitively programmed Socially Programmed Computer, but reprograms other aspects of the computer. The very fact that the therapist can accept the patient as a person worthy of his attention has a strong effect in dampening the excessively self-punitive Socially Programmed Computer.

In child rearing (programming), a positive nonpunitive Self-Conception (Socially Programmed Computer) should be sought, though this can never be totally achieved. The child *does* want to expand. In his heart, the child (like everyone else) does want to put his interests before the interests of society, does want to expand even at the expense of other members of society. Therefore each person has a punitive Self-Conception (Socially Programmed Computer) to some extent. Hence, feelings of guilt and inferiority are universal. The child feels guilt and inferiority because, in his naivety, he assumes that other people are what they appear to be on the surface. He assumes that they are acting only for the good of society, whereas in fact they are only accommodating their needs to society because they will otherwise be destroyed.

Hence the teenager's universal complaint about grown people being false. This complaint means the teenager has become sophisticated enough at this point to realize no one is what he pretends to be, i.e., a thoroughly integrated (programmed) member of society who acts only in the best interests of society. But of course all this is a necessary lie. Normal teenagers recover. Many others grow into radical middle age, still shouting about the false values of the world about them.

The other big objective in child rearing (programming) is to program the child's Socially Programmed Computer so that it helps him express the needs of his Biologically Programmed Computer in positive ways, that is to say, for the benefit of both the individual and society, to express himself through the social institutions which the world provides for such expression. For example, the physically expanding child (physically aggressive) might be programmed for engaging in sports. He might then become a professional baseball player. If, on the other hand, he had considerable intellectual expanding, as well as physically expanding tendencies, he might become a surgeon who specialized in orthopedics. In the specialty of orthopedics (bone surgery) he could manipulate fractures, apply casts, string up splints and in general lead a much more physical existence than the physician who specialized in psychiatry and spends his days sitting behind a desk. Ideally the Socially Programmed Computer is programmed to give the optimal expression of the particular type of Biologically Programmed Computer with which the child is born.

CHAPTER 11

The TOTE Computer

The TOTE Computer (TOTEC) includes Minor and Master problem solving (homeostatic) Plans, the testing of possible routes to achieve homeostasis, the acceptance or rejection of routes for achieving homeostasis and the integration of the Biologically Programmed Computer with the Socially Programmed Computer. Since we have just finished discussing the Biologically Programmed and Socially Programmed Computers, it would seem appropriate first to speak of the integration of the two by the TOTE Computer. Clearly, the Biologically Programmed Computer (BPC) is programmed for the immediate biological needs of the individual without regard to the social needs of the person. Man, being an intensely social animal (because of his early and later great need for his fellow men, his years of childhood dependency) has social needs that are nearly as intense as his biological needs. For this reason his Socially Programmed Computer has been programmed to represent and fulfill these needs without regard to his biological needs.

For successful living a man must have a number of both his biological and social needs met. This is no easy task, considering the fact that these two sets of needs are often in direct conflict with one another. Thus the TOTE Computer's integration of the two sets of needs is of critical importance.

If a hungry man walked past a restaurant and saw the people eating, his Biologically Programmed Computer would tell him to open the door, go inside the restaurant and take the steak from the nearest diner. The problem fed into the BPC would be: hunger. The solution (Minor Plan) given by the BPC would be: eat. Eat now, the first thing you see, smell, hear, or touch which would give you calories to sustain your life.

But if the man rushed into the restaurant, took the steak and ate it, he would find himself in social difficulties. He would be thrown into jail where his "antisocial" inclinations could be restrained and possibly reprogrammed. The Socially Programmed Computer (SPC) could be given the problem:

hunger. The solution it would give: forget about hunger. Try, instead, to find some way to help your fellow man eat. Now, should the man follow the solution given by his SPC, he would stay out of jail, but he would starve to death.

Neither computer has given the man an appropriate solution for his problem: hunger. However, the TOTE Computer (TOTEC) has been programmed with Master and Minor Plans. Furthermore, it has been programmed to solve the man's problem through trial and error in order to fulfill the Master and Minor Plans, just as the TOTEC can be programmed with a Master Plan to win a game of checkers, to remember every move, correct future moves and thus develop into a better checker player. *The Master Plan (MP) in the TOTEC is for the man to attain homeostasis to the greatest possible degree.* Going to jail would not achieve homeostasis for the man. He would be uncomfortable there, isolated from his fellow men and institutions and would not be able to carry out his Expanding Programs. On the other hand, forgetting about the food would leave the man hungry and eventually lead to death. This obviously is not a good solution for his program of homeostasis.

Through trial and error the TOTEC has been programmed to handle this hunger problem. Perhaps in a kindergarten the child tried to take food from a fellow student, only to be frustrated in his attempts by the teacher. "No, you're not to take Johnny's cake," the teacher said, thus foiling the BPC's plan to get food directly. "Finish your painting," the teacher may have said, "and then I'll give you some cake." Thus the TOTEC through trial and error learned that it was possible to carry out the plan presented by the BPC in a manner which would be also acceptable to the plan of the SPC.

Solution programmed into the TOTEC: perform a socially approved act for the teacher and then you will be given your cake. The child finishes his painting and receives his cake. Through trial and error the TOTEC has been programmed to integrate the needs of the BPC and the SPC and attain the maximum homeostasis.

To return to the man on the street whose BPC tells him the solution to his hunger is stealing food, we find that his plan is rejected by the TOTEC which tells him he will be sent to jail if he takes the food from the restaurant diner. The solution to the problem of hunger is furnished by the TOTEC: use some of the money which you earned at work (for performing a socially useful function) and buy food for yourself from the man who owns the restaurant. Thus the man's biological and social needs are both satisfied. The BPC and the SPC are both overridden by the TOTEC which gives a realistic solution to the problem which is in keeping with the Master Plan: homeostasis, both biological and social.

Now that we have seen the TOTEC in action we can understand its testing, accepting or rejecting a possible plan of action, its integration of the plans presented by the BPC and the SPC so that the Master Plan for the individual is served: homeostasis. A few examples illustrate Master and Minor Plans that exist within the TOTEC.

The Master Plan in each individual's TOTEC is to:

1. Survive biologically.
2. Expand biologically.
3. Survive socially.
4. Expand socially.

The details of this Master Plan vary somewhat from age to age, but the Plan remains the same until old age is reached. Even in old age it lives on, though the energies in old age are greatly reduced and so the Plans are not pursued with much vigor.

The newborn infant feeds from his bottle, grows physically in size and power. He attempts very early in life to master his mother and father and anyone else with whom he has social contacts. At the same time he tries with smiles and coos to stay within the good graces of his mother and others in the immediate family.

The young man goes to college while living on food from home as he attempts to learn facts that will serve him for expanding and feeding needs in later life. In order to meet these goals his social behavior must stay within certain bound, otherwise the school authorities will expel him. He attempts to make friends and expand his inter-college social powers according to his abilities.

He sees a pretty coed walk across the campus. His BPC says: "Take her here and now." His SPC says: "Introduce yourself to her but only ask if you can help her with her homework." His TOTEC says: "You may have her but you must court her in an acceptable manner. When you do finally seduce her you must use caution lest you impregnate her. A pregnant coed at this time in your life would only interfere with your Master Plan."

Minor Plans would run something like this: On the first date with the coed (problem for the computer: how to seduce her in a socially acceptable way without interfering with the Master Plan: graduation from college) he might take her to a baseball game and discover she did not care for sports. On the next date he would take her out to dinner and to the theater. He discovers she enjoys dinner and the theater and is much more nearly available to him after the experience. His behavior would then be modified in accordance with his time and finance. If possible he would continue taking her out to dinner and the theater as long as she grew more and more receptive toward his advances. Thus the TOTEC modifies Minor Plans through trial and error, but always keeps in mind the Master Plan which supercedes each Minor Plan.

Again we have the computer playing checkers. Master Plan: to win the game. Minor Plan: to take as many of the opponent's men as possible without losing your own men. Through trial and error the Minor Plan proceeds, always subservient to the Master Plan to win the game.

CHAPTER 12

Chemical Reaction

We must recollect that all our provisional ideas in psychology will some day be based on an organic structure. This makes it probable that special substances and special chemical processes control the operation.

Sigmund Freud

Man = machine + energy + communicator + homeostasis + computer + chemical reaction.

Man is an energized machine with a computer which allows him to achieve homeostasis through the use of communicators. Man is a chemical reaction.

A digital computer is composed of chemical compounds, but they are in a more stable form than the chemical compounds which make up man. Still, the digital computer is not immune to chemical change. A computer designed to function in an air-conditioned building would be so chemically altered by an environment filled with sulphuric acid that it would fail to function. If a teaspoonful of baking soda is dropped into a glass of vinegar, we can readily observe a chemical reaction, a change of state. The compounds react to form new compounds, the whole mass fizzles and bubbles as it moves about in the chemical act of recombining.

Man is, among other things, a skin full of chemicals. While the patient sits across the desk from the therapist his chemistry ticks merrily (or, more likely, depressingly) along. Before coming to the therapist's office the patient felt anxiety. This caused adrenalin to shoot into his blood stream, made him even more tense. The adrenalin made his blood sugar rise. The rise in blood sugar called forth an extra supply of insulin, which brought the blood sugar down to the point where the patient experienced hunger and the tension that accompanies a low blood sugar. Just before entering the office he ate a candy bar. Now his blood sugar is shooting up again. He feels less restless but the elevated blood sugar is bringing forth more insulin to bring the blood sugar down again.

Now he is thirsty because his blood viscosity has increased and his restlessness is increasing again because of the thirst. Instead of listening to the therapist, his mind is on the drinking fountain at work. "I'm sorry, but I'm so thirsty I can't concentrate on what you are saying," the patient might remark. After the therapist gives the patient a drink of water, the patient reaches a temporary homeostasis in his body chemistry, is less tense, and therefore is in a better position to be reprogrammed. All of the hundreds of millions of chemical reactions which are occurring in this patient affect his computer.

In a general book such as this it would be inappropriate to deal with all the known chemistry of the central nervous system; however, in order to illustrate the importance of the practical problem of programming and reprogramming man's computer, a segment of the chemistry (the hardware) of the computer is touched upon. As an illustration we return to the man with hallucinating from LSD who was mentioned in Chapter 1. The reader will recall that this man could not be programmed through behavioral therapy because his computer (hardware) was so disturbed chemically that it was out of touch with reality.

Exactly how memory occurs in the human computer is not known, but a good deal of evidence now points to the fact that memory units are chemical changes which take place within the brain cells. Four reasons lead chemists to believe ribonucleic acid (RNA) guides these chemical changes within the cell: 1. Upon stimulation of the cell, the RNA within the cell changes. 2 RNA within the cell changes after the animal learns. 3. Any reduction of the RNA reduces learning ability. 4. Increased amounts of RNA increases the ability to learn. Thus we might conclude that the cells of the brain undergo chemical changes when they are programmed.

It is now believed that each cell can hold only a small portion, or unit, of the programmed material. These cells are connected one to another in various combinations in order to fill memory programs which are needed for complex behavior. We have, in effect, a network of tiny beads (cells) connected with one another through various combinations of relays (neural tracts). By and large the effectiveness of the computer depends upon having memory cells intact and in communication with other memory cells. The total effect of the various connections produces a behavior pattern. Part of the computer (brain) can be impaired, either destroyed physically or made chemically inoperative, by incapacitating some of the cells or by interfering with the communication system which connects a particular set of cells together to form a particular behavior pattern. In spite of an injury, the behavior system can still operate at a lower rate of efficiency, unless a certain critical point of destruction is passed.

This conception of the total effect of the computer might be compared to the activation of a TV picture tube. A spot on the cathode-ray viewing tube is activated by a stream of electrons, the force of which can be made to vary by the use of a grid. Thus the spot can be made brighter or darker. A magnetic deflecting yoke moves the spot about on the screen to sweep out a scanning raster. By this method a spot of varying intensity can be made to move about on the screen. When a number of spots of varying brightness move about on the screen, the eye perceives a moving picture. If the electrons striking the cathode tube are reduced in number, the viewer still sees an image on the screen, though it will be reduced in quality.

If part of man's total computer is inoperative, man can still follow a behavior pattern, though it may be weakened or distorted by the defect. For example, a man may have part of his computer knocked out by overindulging in alcohol at a party. When he initiates the operant behavior pattern needed to get him home, he may experience some difficulties. The car, as a result, may wander from side to side as he drives along the street. He may take a wrong turn and have to repeat part of his route to find his apartment. Once in the building, he may enter the apartment two doors instead of three doors from the elevator and thus find the attainment of his goal postponed again. We see here a partially damaged (hardware) computer at work. If the computer were damaged sufficiently (incapacitated) we would find the man simply sitting asleep in a corner of the room where the party had been given.

The importance of the memory cells of the computer (brain) and the importance of the network (communicators) which connect them into a behavioral pattern cannot be overemphasized. For this reason an illustration of their chemical behavior is given. To clarify this, the reader should be reminded that the cells (nerves) of the central nervous system (the brain and its branches) do not connect directly to one another like the copper wires which conduct electricity through, say, a house. Once the wires from the house are connected to an electrical supply, we need only throw a switch to complete a circuit. For example, to turn on the hall light you connect the light circuit to the main house circuit by throwing a switch which, in effect, causes the two wires to contact one another in order that electrons may pass freely. The cells in the nervous system do not contact one another directly. Rather they are separated by a space called a cleft, a neural cleft or synapse. The impulse is passed from one cell to another by a chemical which leaves one cell, travels through the space (neural cleft) and touches the next cell.

During the past ten years clear-cut evidence has accumulated that the catecholamines (dopamine and norepinephrine) act as chemical transmitters from cell to cell in the part of the brain which deals with emotions. As a neurotransmitter, norepinephrine, for example, passes through the cell membrane of the nerve ending of one nerve, through the synaptic cleft (which separates the nerve cells) and stimulates the cell body of the next nerve cell.

We are now at the very heart of psychochemotherapy. It is at the point of transmission of a stimulation from one nerve to another that nature may produce defective hardware in the computer of man and thus produce an emotionally or mentally ill person. It is at this point that the hardware damaged computer must be orthomolecularized (normalized, repaired) chemically in order for behavioral therapy (programming) to proceed in a normal manner.

What are some of the defects possible? To start with, norepinephrine may *not* be formed in the nerve cell in a normal manner. It is made from the amino acid tyrosine. Tyrosine is formed from the essential amino acid phenylalanine, but cannot be formed in a person on a diet lacking phenylalanine. On the other hand tyrosine cannot be formed from phenylalanine if the liver is (through a genetic fault in metabolism) deficient in phenylalanine hydroxyglase or if this enzyme is for some reason inactive. Thus, unless tyrosine is present in normal amounts, the neurotransmitter, norepinephrine, cannot be manufactured in the cell in normal amounts, and thus the transmission of excitation from nerve to nerve cannot proceed in a normal manner. We are presented with a hardware damage to the computer.

A child with this brain chemistry defect (defective hardware of its computer) grows up to be abnormal unless immediate steps are taken soon after birth to correct the chemical defect. The child has an abnormal electro-encephalogram, is mentally defective and it is not possible to program him for a normal social life. It is not possible to correctly program an abnormal (hardware damaged) computer. If not permanently damaged, it can be chemically normalized—then programming and reprogramming (psychotherapy) can proceed.

Other defects are possible at the synapse where norepinephrine passes from the tail of one nerve cell to the head of another. The norepinephrine may be destroyed too fast or not fast enough by the enzyme monoamine oxidase, thereby affecting the transmission of impulses from one cell to another. The permeability of cell membranes may be altered. Thus a less permeable cell membrane may be slow to release norepinephrine, whereas a more permeable cell membrane may release it too fast.

When psychotrophic drugs such as imipramine hydrochloride (Tofranil) are administered, the cell membrane is made less permeable to the absorption of the norepinephrine which lies in the synaptic cleft. Hence the norepinephrine is left free to act for a longer time, to excite the receiving nerve cell longer. In this manner a patient who is depressed (has damage to the hardware of his computer) may be normalized by administering imipramine hydrochloride and thus making more norepinephrine available for the passage of nerve impulses.

A patient who is so depressed that he can only sit in his room and stare at the wall cannot be programmed properly. If his computer is normalized chemically, then programming and reprogramming can proceed.

Reserpine (a tranquilizer) reduces the available norepinephrine within the synaptic cleft by causing it to leak out of the vesicals within which it is held inside the nerve cell. When the norepinephrine leaks out of the vesicals it is then deaminated (deactivated) by the enzyme monoamine oxidase. It then leaves the cell in its deactivated form so that when it passes through the synaptic cleft and contacts the next nerve cell, no stimulation occurs. Other tranquilizers are thought to act in a similar manner, though the precise details of their chemical actions have not yet been fully worked out.

A patient, like one suffering from delirium tremens, who is hyperactive to the point of disorientation, cannot be programmed with the usual behavioral techniques. However, if he is first chemically normalized, his computer can be programmed and reprogrammed in the usual fashion.

Transmission at the neural cleft and the general chemical intactness of the neurons are complex matters which may be altered by many factors. We have mentioned that the glucose available to the neuron has a great effect upon its excitability. By extreme variations in the glucose level either coma or excitability can be produced in the organism. The fundamental change is at the level of the neural cleft. The sodium pump, which controls the potassium and sodium levels of the cell, can have an enormous influence upon the activities of the organism.

Certainly vitamins are important in maintaining the intactness of the membrane (*Science News*, May 28, 1970, p. 510) and it has long been known that proper levels of calcium and magnesium are needed for normal neural transmission. Since hormone levels help govern the values for potassium, sodium, calcium, and magnesium, then we begin to understand the complexity of the problem. Certainly the cell membrane cannot function normally unless the proper foods (proteins, vitamins, minerals, trace metals, etc.) are ingested.

Recently the author ran a series of two hundred hair tests on patients. In this test the hair sample was activated by neutrons to obtain readings on the content of copper, magnesium, iron, manganese, calcium, sodium, potassium, and zinc. Most of the figures returned were appalling in their abnormality, almost as appalling as the diets reported by many psychiatric patients. At present he is in the act of supplying the low elements to patients. The improvement in a number of cases has been dramatic. He expects many other patients to improve after several months of correct supplements.

The author knows a man who fights pit bulldogs. He has told him that the meanest, most intractable dogs, those which fight best in the pit, are usually owned by mountaineers who feed their dogs miserable diets: a few pieces of corn bread, a little fat back with a streak or two of pork. As long as the dogs manage to get enough food, vitamins and minerals to stay alive, they are great fighters.

Sometimes when watching TV news programs of rioting the author wonders what these people have been eating. He would like to go among them and get hair tests, vitamin levels, complete nutritional surveys. It is his opinion that they have been living on empty calories from highly processed foods, which are rich in carbohydrates, inexpensive, and easily stored—like bottle drinks and candy bars—which go far toward satisfying the immediate hunger of the individual but in reality leave him starving for essential proteins, vitamins and minerals. These foods leave the person with abnormal neurons, and with cell membranes which cannot respond in the normal manner.

For the first time in history we have a civilization where the average dog has a better diet than the average man. It would be ironic if this civilization fell because of a shortage of a few milligrams of essential food elements in the individual diets of its citizens. Fantastic? Not at all, because mankind hates to admit that he is an animal and therefore dependent upon his chemistry, which in turn is dependent both upon his diet and his particular inherited enzyme patterns.

Of course many other chemical processes are taking place in the brain, but only a few examples can be cited to illustrate the thesis. The question arises whether or not the use of tranquilizers and antidepressants should be considered a part of orthomolecular psychiatry (Pauling has omitted them). True, if a man is suffering from scurvy and therefore depressed, and is given, say, imipramine hydrochloride to improve the symptoms of depression, then the antidepressant is masking the symptom and not curing the underlying cause of the disease.

The author's hair studies have convinced him that antidepressants and tranquilizers are at present *very* widely used to relieve symptoms of mineral and trace element deficiencies. It is theoretically possible, however, that an individual might inherit an enzyme pattern which shows an abnormality at the cell membrane level which might not be corrected by proper diet and proper hormonal control. In this instance an antidepressant or a tranquilizer might act as a true normalizer, might correct the fundamental defect and therefore should be considered a part of orthomolecular therapy. In any case, the author chooses to think of psychochemicals in this manner because he feels that one day the deficiencies will be checked routinely by all competent physicians much as they today test for hemoglobin levels in the blood and albumen in the urine.

To complicate the chemical picture of the computer, it must be realized that the total masses of chemical action depend upon their physical presence. That is to say if one part of the brain is physically larger than another, then it contains more chemicals to act on the other structures of the brain. As pointed out earlier, very many of the chemical reactions taking place in the body generally affect the brain cells. The synapse is stimulated, for example, if the blood sugar falls to a low level. On the other hand, if the blood sugar falls to a very low level, sedation, even to the point of coma and death occurs.

To further complicate the picture, the cells and synapses of the brain (hardware) are affected by the environment. If, for example, a rat is raised in a normal environment and a second rat is raised in total darkness, the visual centers of the brain in the rat raised in darkness will fail to develop properly. This lack of development is so striking that it is possible to sacrifice the rats, examine the visual centers of the brain beneath a microscope and designate which rat was reared in darkness and which one in a normal environment.

At this point the general reader has some idea of the complexity of the problem the therapist faces when a patient walks in, seats himself across the desk and says: "I'm nervous and depressed. What can you do to help me?"

CHAPTER 13

Individuality

Man = machine + energy + computer + homeostasis + communicator + chemical reaction + individuality.

Man is an energized machine with a computer which allows him to achieve homoeostasis through the use of communicators. He is a chemical reaction and is highly individualistic.

A casual stroll through any city reveals the physical differences in the people one passes on the street: tall, short, medium height. Indeed, if a sensitive enough measuring device were used it would undoubtedly be discovered that every person in the world is of a different height. Not only is each person of a different height, but the height of the individual varies within certain limits. In the morning, for example, after lying in bed all night, a person is taller than he is at night. Even the hydration of a man changes his height. Hence if he drinks a glass of water, his height changes. The height of most people, like all other measurements, follows a normal curve. Most people are between five and six feet in height. A few are less than five feet and a few over six feet. Variations in every physical measurement could be demonstrated: nose, lips, eyes, color, etc.

What we do not realize so readily is that each man has a central nervous system (the hardware of the computer) different from every other. The thickness of the cortex, the size of the frontal lobes, and the size of the thalamic nuclei, to name a few, vary from individual to individual. Add the chemical differences in the hardware of the computers from man to man and we have a more complete picture of individuality. If the acidity of the skin or the acidity of the stomach is tested, it is apparent that each individual varies in all his chemical attributes.

The chemistry of the brain differs from person to person. The permeability of the membranes of the brain cells vary from one person to the next, as well as the total amount of norepinephrine. Metabolic differences exist from brain to brain, thus altering the action of norepinephrine and the other catechol-amines in the brain which control neurotransmission of impulse from brain cell to brain cell. Thus, not only is the hardware of every computer different but each of them has been programmed in a somewhat different way, both bio-logically and socially. Every human computer is only relatively normal or relatively abnormal. The normality and abnormality blend imperceptibly into the other.

The now classic experiment of Tryon illustrates the importance of inheritance in forming the hardware of the computer. Tryon took a group of 142 rats and tested them for maze-learning ability. He then separated the rats into two groups. The first groups consisted of rats which learned quickly to run the maze correctly. The second group was composed of rats which slowly learned to run the maze correctly. He then inbred each group separately. In Fig. 1 it can be seen that marked differences in maze-learning ability exist in the seventh generation of rats so bred. Although the rat's BPC was not, strictly speaking, born with a full program for maze running, still the BPC and the hardware was formed in such a way that some rats *could easily* be programmed for maze running and the other rats *could not* be easily programmed for maze running.

At this point we reach a highly emotionally charged topic which is usually skipped by the prudent scientist. Nevertheless, mankind must not be ruled by his emotions, and surely the field of science cannot allow itself to be restricted by passing passions. A few thousand years from now emotions concerning the races of mankind will surely have passed on, but the principles of science will still live. Two plus three will still equal five. Hopefully there will be earthlings about to make the observation.

Since each individual has a different hardware and software from his neighbor, surely it would be reasonable to expect differences between races. Lest anyone should take offense, the author would like to say firstly that he does not look upon any particular traits of any particular race as being superior to those of another. The word "superior" suggests a value judge-ment. Therefore, to talk in terms of superior or inferior one must ask: inferior or superior in what manner?

Obviously if we judge in terms of ability to withstand the onslaught of the sun's rays in a lifeboat in the tropics, we find the Negro superior to the Caucasian, since his skin is chemically better suited to resisting the harmful rays of the sun. If we judge superiority in terms of resistance to malaria, the Negro wins again, because his body is chemically better able to resist the infection than the body of a Caucasian. If we judge superiority or inferiority in terms of resistance to tuberculosis, the Caucasian usually is

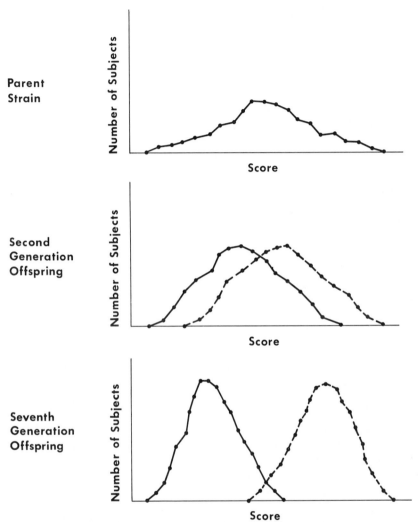

Fig. 1. Results of selective breeding for a behavioral trait which is polygenically inherited. ----- Offspring of High Scorers, ———Offspring of Low Scorers. (Adapted from Tryon.)

considered superior in this particular instance. The author wishes to make no claims as to general superiority or inferiority of the races, only to point out they must of necessity differ chemically. Reason would indicate that the chemical differences extend beyond the chemistry of the skin.

The author can only hope that he will not be quoted out of context by persons furthering their own particular beliefs.

In summary, each man differs chemically from every other man, this chemical difference is inherited, and it is reasonable to suppose that people of similar inheritance are more likely to be chemically alike that people who have no common inheritance.

Stodolsky and Lesser of Harvard University have recently published an interesting paper on the *particular* mental differences between several ethnic groups. Figure 2 illustrates the findings from their study.

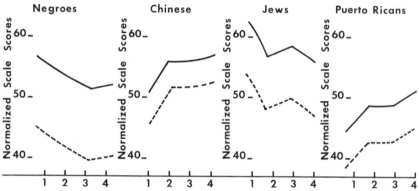

Fig. 2. Ethnic groups show distinctive patterns of mental ability; curves within each group run parallel regardless of class. ——— Middle Class; - - - - Lower Class. (Reproduced from *Science News*, Vol. 93, 20 April, 1968.

It will be noted that both the middle class and the low class individuals from the ethnic groups displayed the same patterning of particular intelligence. This is evidence of differences among the ethnic groups for differences in their computers.

Great emotional turmoil followed William B. Shockley's (Nobel Prize winner in physics, 1956) talk before the National Academy of Science in which he pointed out that in all likelihood slum dwellers perpetuated themselves through the genetic passage of traits which placed their children at a disadvantage when it came to competition in the particular society in which they wished to compete. He stated that for humanitarian reasons, if for none other, this problem should be given priority for investigation; that scientific investigation should replace emotionalism in this area. Surely this was a reasonable request.

When a person's computer deviates a great deal from the median, it is said to be abnormal. This abnormality of the computer can occur as a result of a physical or chemical damage, or malformation of the hardware (central nervous system), or of the software (programming—BPC or SPC). Of course many inherited chemical disorders result in damage to the hardware of the computer. Among the better known are Downer's syndrome, PKU, and cretinism.

The high rate of schizophrenia in certain families has long been a clinical observation, but a well-controlled study of this genetic (computer hardware) defect was not published until Kallmann made his studies known in 1946 and 1950. His statistics were concentrated upon 953 schizophrenic twins. Quite clearly he pointed out that schizophrenia is an inherited disorder, hence is most basically a chemical disorder in which the patient has a computer with abnormal (chemically malformed) hardware, or an abnormal Biologically Programmed Computer.

Two egg twins developed a concordance rate for schizophrenia of 14.7. This was very close, as would be expected, to the full sibling rate of 14.3. As expected the half sibling rate was 7.1. With single egg twins, however, the concordant rate leaped up to a statistically conclusive level of 85.8. Quite clearly these figures should settle the question about which is the more important—heredity (hardware and the Biologically Programmed Computer) or environment (software), in the production of the mental illness known as schizophrenia.

L. L. Heston, in the August 1966 issue of the *Journal of British Psychiatry* reported, in a careful study, on 47 babies of schizophrenic mothers. These babies were placed in normal homes immediately after birth. Still, half of the babies showed marked mental abnormalities. This included mental deficiency, schizophrenia, criminality, and discharge from armed services for psychiatric behavioral reasons.

A study has come from the University of Iowa in which identical twin children of schizophrenic mothers in Puerto Rico were separated from the mothers at birth and reared in separate environments. A very high percentage of each twin developed schizophrenia.

Early sensory deprivation was once put forward as the cause for schizophrenia. This seems to have been repudiated by another study which showed the incidence of schizophrenia among congenitally deaf persons to be no higher than in the general population.

Sandor Rado, one of Freud's disciples, has spent his life confirming the biological etiology of schizophrenia and manic-depressive psychosis. In manic-depressives he found a tendency toward overreaction in affective areas, a persistent oral dependence state, a strong need for external gratification, and an intolerance to pain. These traits had been present in his patients from infancy. Rado also reported in manic-depressives a genetic similarity to Kallmann's schizophrenics in twin studies. Kallmann reported an almost 100% concordance rate of homosexuality in one egg twins, whereas with two egg twins the rate of homosexuality was no more than that found in the general population.

Investigations in the area of criminality have revealed that this trait appears in a concordant rate of 14% in opposite sex pairs, 54% in same sex two egg pairs and 66% in one egg pairs, demonstrating the importance the inherited aspect of the computer plays in the production of criminals. In Scotland it has been recently discovered that an inherited defect in the Y chromosome occurs sixty times more frequently in the population of criminals confined to prison than in the population generally. This is strong evidence for the inheritance of abnormal hardware, which exerts a marked effect upon behavior because computers with damaged hardware cannot be successfully programmed.

In the field of psychological tests more evidence has been accumulated concerning the inheritance of a computer with malformed Biologically Programmed Computer or hardware. For example, Gottesman found a strong genetic component, as evidenced in Minnesota Multiphasic Personality Inventory family profiles, in anxiety, depression, obsession, and schizoid withdrawal.

CHAPTER 14

The Box

Man = machine + energy + computer + communicator + homeostasis + chemical reaction + individuality + box.

Man is an energized machine with a computer which uses a communicator to receive and send information to achieve homeostasis. He is a highly individualistic chemical reaction and lives in a box.

A box is not required for the programming of the Biologically Programmed Computer. The programming of this computer is genetically determined. However, for the Socially Programmed Computer to become programmed, it is necessary to have the computer confined in an operant stimulus-response behavioral structure.

We return to the Skinner box mentioned in Chapter 1, where the mouse lived in a box and pressed a lever to obtain food. All of us live in a Skinner box, though we do not admit it. The author, for example, travels from his apartment (compartment #1 of his box) over streets (compartment #2) to his office (compartment #3) six days a week, where he helps people with their emotional problems (presses the bar, so to speak) and in return receives his reward (money) which he can use for food, clothing, shelter, security, and toys (rewards). It is true that he sometimes escapes his box for short periods of time on vacations, but at least 95% of his life is spent within his box, pressing his bar for rewards. But, of course, bar pressing for rewards within a box is what life is all about. Some people have referred to it as work. These acts which people perform for rewards get the buildings built, the sick doctored, the taxes collected.

One might say that much of child rearing (programming the young) consists of getting them to eventually press a bar (work) for a reward (money). If the mouse is given food (a reward) without pressing the bar, he will never become programmed for bar pressing. If a mouse is not confined to the Skinner box (is allowed to wander over to the other side of the laboratory and eat crumbs from beneath the sink) he will not become programmed for bar pressing. If a child is not kept in his Skinner box (sometimes referred to as a school) and trained to press the bar (pass tests) for rewards (love and prestige) he will not become properly programmed for adult bar pressing in his adult Skinner box (home and work).

As dreary as this life of bar pressing in a box might sound, we humans have become more or less adjusted to it. Millions of years of foraging and hunting for food has conditioned us for work. Indeed what is one to do for eight hours a day, day after day, if not struggle for food? A reporter once asked William Faulkner why he wrote so much. "What," he replied in effect, "are you going to do eight hours a day, week after week, if not work? You can't drink eight hours a day, day after day, and you can't make love eight hours a day, day after day. What is left except work?" Indeed we complain about work because we harbor the idea that leisure is sweet, but the most miserable patients the author deals with (and those often most difficult to help) are those who do not need to work to support themselves.

The Humanistic Revolution has dominated much of the Western World's thinking during the past several hundred years. It has been an attempt to glorify and enhance the dignity of man and to free him from the ironbound social traditions of the Middle Ages. Humanism has more or less ignored Darwin, however, and has sought to color man with a nobility which he does not have. The Humanistic Revolution, by ignoring man's biological self, has tried to pretend that man is good and kind, that he is so good that he gives charity to all the poor, leniency to every lawbreaker. On the other hand, while he denies his innate aggression and the fact that he too is subject to evolutionary forces, man develops the arts of war so that they consume a very large part of his productivity and uses these arts of war to kill millions in "justifiable wars."

Has not the Humanistic Revolution, by ignoring man's biological roots, turned man into a schizophrenic creature who gives bread with his left hand while he sows death and destruction with his right hand? Humanism perpetuates a cruel lie when it says that love solves everything, that man is free, that each person is born equal, that humans are important in the evolutionary vastness of space and time. In the long run, Mother Nature plays no favorites. Neither is she sentimental. She does not spend time weeping over the passing of the dinosaur, any more than she would mourn the passing of man. But, more important to the present discussion is the fact that the Humanistic Revolution has shouted freedom so loud and strong that people have come to believe in the delusion that mankind is free, that he does not, or should not, live in a Skinner box.

In the opinion of the author, one of the greatest mistakes mankind has made in following his concept of Humanism is in the changes he has made in his child-rearing techniques. Man, in his false pursuit of freedom, has removed much of the box in which a child must live in order to be properly programmed for his own and society's best interest. "You shouldn't frustrate children," people, who have called themselves liberal educators, have been shouting at every possible opportunity.

Only by placing a child in a box, where he is frustrated, where he must make behavioral choices, can he be properly programmed. Only by placing a child in a box where he must satisfy his needs through proper channels (bar pressing) can he be programmed. Some of the present freedom for children stems from a popular misinterpretation of Freud. He, correctly, said that emotional difficulties were in part caused by frustrations of childhood desires. Here the popular educator stopped reading. If the educator had read farther he would have learned that Freud felt that frustration was an essential part of growing up, that children needed to learn to deal with frustrations, to internally handle some of the frustrations and to find socially approved outlets for part of his frustration. Thus, in reality, Freud was in favor of placing the child, as well as the patient, in a box. The limit setting that the parent establishes for the child forms the child's box. If a rat is left to run free in an unlimited, unstructured environment, his computer will become programmed, but not in an orderly, predetermined manner.

Child rearing is an act of programming the SPC. For the child to be programmed correctly then, he must be kept in a box, so to speak. The child who is ignored by his programmers (parents) is out of his programming box and is not being programmed. If a child is allowed to eat mashed potatoes with his hands and the mother does not reinforce his using a fork (by rewarding fork-using activity with love and attention), he will continue to eat mashed potatoes with his hands, unless he is later programmed for better eating habits by his peers.

If a teenage child is allowed to run loose on the streets, to live outside of his box, then he will not be programmed in the box known as a school. He will become, like the rat, haphazardly programmed by his contacts with the wider environment, and by the people whom he happens to meet in that environment. "You're chicken," one of his peers might say when the boy declines to steal a car. To prove that he is not "chicken" (to get the approval of his peers) the boy will then join his peers in a car stealing act. Because he receives reinforcement (approval) for this activity, he is being programmed by his peers to steal automobiles. Clearly his SPC is being programmed for antisocial activity which is not in his best interest.

The reprogrammer (psychotherapist) faces a similar problem when he takes on the task of reprogramming a person who has not been acting in his own best interest, either because of neurotic, psychotic or antisocial behavior. Many therapists fail in their reprogramming attempts because they do not place their patient in a box. Freud stated that a certain stability of character was required before psychoanalysis could be effective. This was his way of saying that a patient must voluntarily stay in a box if he is going to come to grips with his problems, to allow himself to become reprogrammed. If the patient is acting out his problems (for example, making love not only to his wife but also to his secretary and the woman next door) then it is impossible to program his expanding drives into directions which are most beneficial to him. The same is true if he flits from job to job or refuses to become involved with the world. If the therapist has a patient who simply lies around his apartment all day in a semidrunken stupor, obviously this patient is not allowing himself to stay in the box needed for reprogramming. To be reprogrammed, the patient must allow himself to go out into the box of the world so that, by trial and error, he can become programmed.

Alcohol, marihuana, etc., even in small amounts, are the great box melters. They allow people to escape. Instead of engaging in bar pressing activities for food, the intoxicated mouse sits in the corner of his box happily oblivious to his hunger. To hell with bar pressing and rewards! Clearly, an alcohol-happy mouse (or man) cannot be programmed or reprogrammed.

Unfortunately the public tends to equate tranquilizers with alcohol, marihuana, etc. "Why take a tranquilizer? That just covers over my problems," a patient may say, or feel. Alcohol does keep people from coming to grips with their problems, does allow them to escape from the behavioral box. But, on the contrary, tranquilizers in the proper doses act in an entirely different manner. Many agree that the word tranquilizer was an unfortunate choice of terminology for the newer psychotrophic drugs. Normalizer would be a much more appropriate name. For, in fact, the newer psychotrophic drugs normalize the computer rather than simply tranquilize it. A tranquilizer, unlike alcohol, does not allow a patient to escape from the box.

PART II

Therapeutic Implications

CHAPTER 15

Psychotherapy

It is the basic premise of this book that man is, for psychological purposes, a computer, and that this computer can fail to function properly if the hardware (central nervous system) is physically or chemically damaged or if the software (Biologically Programmed Computer or Socially Programmed Computer) is abnormal.

It follows then that, if damaged or abnormal, the computer must be, in so far as possible, normalized (orthomolecularized) with psychochemicals before it can be programmed to function effectively. If the computer were programmed incorrectly during childhood (biologically or socially) then it is usually possible to reprogram the computer correctly through the use of behavioral psychotherapy and/or psychochemotherapy.

When the hardware sustains a physical injury, true repair is not possible, since, once destroyed, tissue of the central nervous system is lost. Chemically damaged hardware (such as that of schizophrenics) can often be normalized (repaired) by the use of psychochemicals. The same statements can be made for many computers showing manic-depressive symptoms and personality disorders. However, even with hardware damage, help is not impossible. The brain damaged child can often be helped toward normality with the use of modern psychochemicals. For example, the child who unreasonably explodes into rages following measles encephalitis may be calmed by the use of psychochemicals.

Some computers show evidence of damage to the software. For example, a child might be born with excessively strong Expanding Programs in the Biologically Programmed Computer, which constantly throw him into conflict with his parents. His life will be further complicated if his Biologically Programmed Computer is strong in the direction of Intractability. This child is constantly told by his parents that he is a bad boy. His parents program his

Socially Programmed Computer to be self-punitive, so that the boy grows up to have a negative self-image which tends to turn his Expanding Drives against himself and prevent their healthy expression through the social institutions available to all men.

The child's Expanding Programs and Intractability (damaged BPC) could be normalized (repaired) with the use of tranquilizers at which time his Socially Programmed Computer could be programmed in the normal manner. But psychochemicals are dealt with in the following chapter. The problem to be discussed here is the reprogramming of computers through psychotherapy.

Behavioral psychotherapy can be used for all types of damaged computers, but this form of programming is particularly effective when used in conjunction with a normalizer (psychochemical), or where there is damage only to the software (Socially Programmed Computer).

We have an almost unlimited supply of psychological schools, each of which has its own theory of human development and accompanying theory of psychological treatment for emotional disorders. An encyclopedia could be written on the various schools. To point out their variety, some examples are: Functional Psychology, Associationism, Reflexology, Early Behaviorism, Late Behaviorism, Operant Behaviorism, Gestalt Psychology, Eclectic, Organic, Genetic, Murry's Personalogy, Lewin's Field Theories, Allport's Individual Psychology, and Phenomenology. We could add to this list hypnotherapy (deep and superficial), group psychotherapy, and psychodrama. Then we enter another field where we find Existentialists, Jungians, Neo-Freudians, Roseians, Alderians, Ego-Analysts and Rogersarians, to name only a few.

When statistics are finally arrayed we learn from Pfeiffer, Eysenck, and others, somewhat to the dismay of the neophyte, that about two-thirds of the emotionally ill patients make significant improvement no matter what school his therapist follows. To completely muddy the water it must be added, in all fairness, that about two-thirds of the emotionally disturbed people also improve whether or not they are treated by any therapist!

Here it would seem the author has worked himself out on a limb and chopped it off. But not so, because, as demonstrated later, behavior therapy is an element at work not only in all forms of psychotherapy but also in the world at large to which the disturbed person is exposed.

Here is an example of what might well be happening in the office of a disciple of Carl Rogers' Client-Centered Psychotherapy as he reprograms a "client". "I sometimes wonder if I can keep on living with my mother," the twenty-five-year-old schoolteacher tells her therapist. "You find it a strain living with your mother?" the therapist replies. "It's—I don't know. It's just difficult sometimes. Take last Saturday night. I had a date and was all ready to leave with him to go to a party and Mother had one of her sinking spells. She told us to go on to the party and not bother about her. But. . . well I just couldn't leave her like that." "How did you feel?" "Do you want to know how I really felt?" "Maybe it would be a good idea for us to try to understand how you felt." "Well," the client says and gives a sigh, "well, to be perfectly honest about my feelings, I was put out by her. I know it isn't very nice to feel put out with your mother just because she has a sinking spell, but I just couldn't help being put out." "I wonder if most daughters wouldn't have felt the same thing you felt." "Do you guess they would? Sometimes I think I'm not very grateful to my mother. I can't help but wonder if other women my age feel that way sometimes about their mothers." "That's an interesting question."

What do we see happening? This Rogers' Client-Centered therapist is re-programming his client's Socially Programmed Computer. Specifically, he is reprogramming the Self-Conception compartment of the SPC. By accepting (rewarding with the love and interest of an important person) the client as a worthwhile person in spite of the fact that she has negative feelings toward her mother, the therapist (programmer) is reprogramming the client (SPC) to accept herself as a worthwhile person in spite of her negative feelings. This is clearly behavioral therapy.

Now we might skip to another therapy session with this client. "After my session with you the other day, I made a big decision," the client states. "Oh?" "I decided to join a hiking club." "You joined a hiking club?" "That's right." "Would you like to tell me about it?" "The club meets every other weekend and goes on an overnight hike. There are lots of young people in it my own age." "That sounds interesting." "I'm looking forward to it."

Here the therapist shows interest in his client's broadening social contact, in her seeking to express her Expanding Programs through a socially approved social institution. His interest rewards her new behavior. He is reprogramming her SPC through the use of behavioral techniques, though the therapist would explain his activities in other terms.

Much the same process happens in every form of psychotherapy. Perhaps a Freudian analyst would remain silent, but he would give the patient a return appointment and greet her with his usual smile at the time of her next visit. This would mean that he was continuing to accept her as a worthwhile person. If, on the other hand, the patient returned to the Freudian analyst the next day and told him she had *given up* the idea of joining the hiking club he would say: "I wonder what this means?" And he would continue to analyze the reasons for her change in plans until she did join the hiking club. Thus he is using positive and negative reinforcement just like the Rogersarian.

While the author was in training under Joel Handler, an analyst whom the author considers one of the few really great psychotherapists, he once mentioned a professional woman who was in analysis with him. She had begun having sexual relations with a Chicago hoodlum and was not bothering to use any means of contraception. The therapist was asked how he would manage the problem. Dr. Handler said he was going to analyze her reasons for not using a contraceptive. "What if she keeps having intercourse without using any protection?" "Then I'll keep analyzing her failure to use contraception until she starts using some protection," Handler replied. Clearly this analyst was using behavior therapy.

When the author was an intern on Jules Masserman's service at the University of Chicago in 1945, Metrasol was still being used for convulsive therapy. Anyone who has ever used this agent for producing seizures in psychiatric patients knows that the patients very much hated the treatment. Sometimes not quite enough medication was given to produce a seizure. When this occurred, patients experienced a dreadful subjective feeling which they feared and hated.

When Masserman would make rounds the house staff would follow him into a room where he would ask the patient how he was feeling. The conversation would go something like this: "Pretty good," the patient would say. "You'd better get better fast or we'll have to use some more convulsive therapy on you," Masserman would say. "I'm going to be better." "Did you eat breakfast?" "A little." "You'd better eat a big breakfast tomorrow or you'll get another treatment." "Don't worry. I will." Here Masserman was, of course, using behavior therapy, negative reinforcement, and not very subtle therapy at that.

In a standard psychoanalysis the first few months are spent in what analysts refer to as the "honeymoon." During these months the patient at great length tells the analyst about his life. At first the patient is reluctant to reveal the negative aspects of his life, all the petty actions, feelings and thoughts which occur in every life. But as the patient tests the analyst and learns that he still accepts him as a worthwhile human, the patient confesses more and more material. The analyst abets this process by "uncovering" material of which the patient may not be consciously aware. After bringing out all the personal wash, the patient learns that the analyst still accepts him.

Here, clearly, the analyst is reprogramming the patient's Socially Programmed Computer so that the patient's Self-Conception is improved. "I thought I was such a bastard, but the analyst seems as friendly as ever," the patient concludes, somehow completely forgetting the fact that he is paying the analyst four or five hundred dollars a month to approve of him, to listen to all the material the analyst has heard a hundred times before and which bores him to the point of distraction. The patient is being reprogrammed, however, to accept himself as a worthwhile person. Hence, the patient will be less punitive towards himself in the future.

During this honeymoon period, the patient gradually develops a great dependency upon the analyst, falls in love with him, so to speak, builds him into a giant philosopher who holds all the world's knowledge between his handsome ears. At this point the patient begins to expect more from the analyst. The patient is now giving all his love and attention to the analyst but does not seem to be getting enough love in return.

Sooner or later the patient's growing anger shows itself, usually in the form of a dream. Perhaps the patient has dreamed he is in an airplane trying to shoot King Kong off the Empire State Building. "I wonder who this King Kong represents?" the analyst says. "Well, he's big and powerful and hairy. He's a mean son-of-a-bitch who's trying to tear everything to pieces. I don't like him. I want to shoot him down. Maybe he's my father. What do you think?" "Maybe," the analyst says in a voice which shows he is not satisfied with the answer. "He could be my boss at work. But it's hard to think of Mr. Jones as King Kong. Mr. Jones practically tiptoes around the office and never says anything to me without apologizing first." "It doesn't sound much like Mr. Jones." "Well, Danny Fisher. You know how he's always. . ." "I wonder," the analyst says, "I wonder if *I* might not be King Kong."

At this point the patient denies the interpretation. It is too frightening to think of the analyst as being anything but a god. But the analyst keeps pushing in this area for several days or weeks. The patient goes through a period of agonizing anxiety. "You know I think you were right about King Kong. Maybe I am a little angry with you, but I can't imagine why." Now the patient gradually is allowed to bring out all of the suppressed anger which has been building up toward the analyst. The patient keeps on expressing his anger for months and months until the topic finally dies because the emotion wears out from repetition. This is known as the resolution of the transference neurosis. In spite of all the anger the patient expresses toward the analyst, he still accepts the patient as a worthwhile person.

Here we see the patient's Socially Programmed Computer reprogrammed so that the Self-Conception is altered. No longer does the patient look upon himself as a basically unacceptable human being, nor have to keep punishing himself with fits of depression and maneuvering himself into life situations in which he not only fails but actually has been making himself suffer. In the course of psychoanalysis the patient naturally talks about his current life, as well as his relationship with the analyst. Here the analyst, by rewarding with interest or by withholding interest, encourages the patient to develop outlets for his Expanding Programs through social institutions.

Popular opinion still holds that the main part of an analysis is spent on past life. This is a false conception. Most modern day analysts spend the greater part of the time on current life and the analysis of the transference neurosis. The author, having had a 900-hour personal analysis, feels he can speak with some authority on the subject. Certainly it was time and money well spent, but it was, in effect, behavioral therapy. The author has no wish to degrade psychoanalysts, or any other kind of therapy, as being unacceptable. He only wishes to point out that all forms of psychotherapy are merely variations of behavioral therapy.

What of the more superficial types of therapy? Perhaps a very disturbed patient will present himself to the, say, eclectic psychotherapist. A careful history may make the therapist conclude that the patient is barely holding onto reality, that therapy will be able to do no more than support the patient in his struggle to survive his day to day battles.

The author remembers a dentist who consulted him many years ago. The man was so disturbed that he had copied down passages from the Bible and pasted them on the mirror above the sink where he washed his hands. He would work on a patient's teeth for five or ten minutes, turn away and wash his hands. The real purpose of washing his hands was to give him a chance to read one of the inspirational quotations from the Bible which he had typed out and pasted on the mirror above the sink. "I guess you think I'm pretty silly to read those Bible passages while I'm working," he said. "I don't see anything wrong with reading the Bible if it helps you get through your day," this therapist replied.

Clearly the patient was doing his best to fight off a psychotic break. It was the therapist's duty to reinforce any tags of strength the patient might grab to keep himself from sinking. Thus, in this simple maneuver, the therapist let the patient know that he approved of the patient's attempts to keep his sanity, that the therapist approved of him as a person and would not brand him "silly" the way the Self-Conception part of his SPC was laughing at him. In this way his reprogramming was begun.

In supportive therapy, the therapist is often more direct, less subtle, in handling the process of reprogramming. Also in supportive therapy the therapist readily lends the patient the use of the therapist's computer for decision making. The loan of the therapist's computer (much like "loaning" a pint of blood to an anemic patient from a blood bank) is made in all forms of psychotherapy. This loan is only more apparent during supportive therapy.

At this point the reader will readily perceive that all forms of psychotherapy are in reality various forms of behavioral therapy (stretching all the way from hypnotherapy and psychoanalysis to psychodrama therapy) in which the therapist gives negative or positive reinforcements for the patient's thoughts and actions for the purpose of reprogramming the patient.

Lest the reader get the wrong impression, Self-Conception is by no means the only aspect of the computer which is reprogrammed through psychotherapy. If, for example, a patient has withdrawn from bar pressing activities (work) then the patient must be denied (made hungry, so to speak) in order to begin the reprogramming.

The author once saw a young lady who was suffering from a schizophrenic process characterized by withdrawal. For seven years following graduation from high school she had sat home watching TV. She was placed on appropriate medication which improved her feeling of well being but still did not make her inclined to start bar pressing activities. When all other attempts to get her moving failed, she was told quite frankly that she had a choice to make: either go to work or go to the state mental hospital.

"But this is blackmail! This is coercion!" many people will scream and accuse him of being a heartless doctor. Nonsense. The world gives all of us choices and we simply choose the road which gives us the least total pain. Sometimes when the author gets up in the morning he considers turning over in bed, going back to sleep, and forgetting about his patients. At 7 a.m. he is faced with a choice: either stay home and indulge his desire to sleep longer, or go to work. If he stays home he will lose his self-respect, the respect of other members of society, as well as his income, which means he will lose status, house and car. He chooses to go to work, to press the bar.

So in giving the patient the choice of going to a rather unpleasant hospital or going to work, a situation is simply set up in which she is free to make a choice. The patient (for the first time) cried and called him all kinds of names, but the next week she went to work and has worked ever since. In addition, she has started singing lessons and hopes to enter college next year to become a music teacher. Now she fully realizes the value of neo-behavioral orthomolecular psychiatry.

A "kind" doctor would have allowed this patient to sit home for the rest of her life, but in so doing he would have contributed to her illness. In all probability she would never have "worked through" her problems and gone to work without being pushed into a behavioral situation. Her fear was too great to break the work barrier unless pushed to do so.

Before leaving this section a few words would seem to be in order regarding behavioral therapy as it is often practiced. In the author's view, it seems naively preoccupied with the eradication of symptoms, to the neglect of the whole patient. Before beginning behavioral therapy, the therapist should, in his opinion, first make a thorough psychological and biochemical study of the patient. If any significant depth of psychopathology or chemopathology discovered, then the patient should first be orthomoleculized insofar as possible prior to the beginning of (or at least concomitantly with) behavioral therapy.

For example, the author is now seeing a young woman who spent almost ten years intermittently addicted to heroin. Psychological tests and clinical examinations showed that she was essentially schizophrenic. Because she was so very ill when she first consulted him and because he was handling her on an outpatient basis, he had to begin therapy without his customary battery of chemical tests.

He assumed she was hypoglycemic (since at least 90% of patients presenting her clinical picture are) and assumed she was low on vitamin B-12. A hair test revealed she was low in calcium and sodium. These low values are frequently accompanied by hypoglycemia. The low sodium most often goes along with borderline hypoadrenalcorticism (Tintera's syndrome).

Her present medication consists of: niacin (20 gms. daily), ascorbic acid (3 gms. daily), Ca plus (a protein chelated calcium compound—three times daily), Regus tablet (a multiple vitamin, multiple mineral supplement—three times daily), conjugated estrogens (1.2 mg., 21 days out of 28 days), diazepam (5 mgs., five times daily), desipramine hydrochloride (25 mgs. three times daily), and amitriptyline hydrochloride (50 mgs. at bedtime). In addition to this, three times weekly, she receives intravenously, 1000 mcgs. of whole adrenal cortex extract mixed with benadryl (50 mgs.), B-12 (1000 mcgs.), and pyridoxine (50 mgs.).

This may seem like an heroic amount of medication, but it is quite common in a practice such as the author's where he prefers to deal with persons suffering from severe forms of what he considers desperate chemical illnesses. He has now started this patient on behavioral conditioning with the use of carbon dioxide. The patient is making quite satisfactory progress considering the fact that she has been working with him for only two months. If, however, he had started out by using behavioral therapy without first taking steps to orthomolecularize her, he feels the whole project would have failed in short order.

He has treated dozens of patients with phobias in the old days using psychotherapy only. Now he uses chemotherapy plus behavior therapy. Much better results are obtained at less expense with the newer method.

Wolpe has reported excellent results with the use of classical symptom oriented behavioral therapy, but others have not been able to repeat his successes. Using a control group treated with conventional psychotherapy against a group treated with classical behavioral therapy at the Maudsley Hospital in London, Cooper concluded that about the same results were obtained with each method of therapy.

Again we return to the old two-thirds rule: no matter how emotionally disturbed patients are treated, indeed, even if they are not treated at all, two-thirds of them show significant improvement. Only by adding orthomolecular therapy to behavior therapy do we push the improvement above the two-thirds rate. Earlier the author promised to return to the two-thirds of the patients who improved without any therapy and to show how they were re-programmed by their contacts with "life," with the normal reinforcements people meet within the box where they live.

Let us return once more to the patient who was being treated by a thera-pist trained in Rogers' Client-Centered psychotherapy. The reader will recall the young lady who lived with a mother who had "sinking spells" when her daughter started out on a date. It will be recalled that the therapist began reprogramming her by showing that he approved of her even though she did feel vexed with her mother. The therapist also encouraged the girl's expressing her Expanding Programs by joining a hiking club where she would, possibly, meet a young man who would help her further fulfill her other Expanding Programs, i.e., reproduction.

Instead of going to a therapist the young lady might well have talked her problem over with an aunt. "I don't know what to do about Mother," she might have said. "Every time I go out on a date, she has a sinking spell. She's driving me to distraction." "If you ask me," the aunt might well reply, "I'd say your mother was just pretending to be sick so she could keep you home. She's afraid you'll get married and leave her." "I imagine that's just what happens. I hate to hurt her, still. . . ." "Take my advice and ignore your mother. She'll live through it." "I hate to hurt her." "You've got your life ahead of you. If you sit home with her till she passes on, you'll be too old for any man to ask you for dates. Life will have passed you by."

Here we see a young lady being reprogrammed by a normal social contact in nearly the same manner she would have been reprogrammed by a therapist. The aunt accepts the girl as a worthwhile person in spite of the girl's negative feelings toward her mother. Thus the SPC, Self-Conception part, is being re-programmed. The girl is also being reprogrammed to continue her Expanding Programs in a socially approved manner, that is to say she is being re-programmed to continue dating, and all that dating implies, in spite of her mother's neurotic attempts to keep her home. The young lady in the normal course of events surrounding her life is being reprogrammed so that she will tend to recover from her emotional problem. She might easily have been reprogrammed by seeing a TV play in which the heroine had a problem with her clinging mother and solved the problem by overthrowing her mother.

The young lady might have given in to her mother, remained at home, given up the man who tried to date her. In this case, the girl might have brooded so much over giving up her Expanding Programs that she would suffer a great deal. The next time a man asked her to go out on a date, the young lady might have accepted. She would then brood over having overthrown her mother, but the brooding and pain might have been less than on the occasion when she surrendered to her mother. Thus the young lady, in seeking homeostasis, might have chosen the lesser pain and continued to date the man in spite of her mother's maneuvering.

In such simple ways life tends to be a learning experience in which people are constantly being reprogrammed. Just as the body tends to cure itself in time and reach homeostasis, so the computer tends to reprogram itself for better health as time passes. Unsuccessful attempts at living (neurotic and psychotic mechanisms for reaching homeostasis) tend to be given up in favor of more effective actions for achieving homeostasis (the expression of the Biologically Programmed Computer and the Socially Programmed Computer through social institutions). The whole process is usually speeded up by the use of psychochemicals. Indeed a satisfactory recovery is often not possible for seriously ill people without the use of psychochemicals to first normalize the computer.

CHAPTER 16

Psychochemotherapy

Until 1955 the population of mental hospitals relative to the general population increased every year. Neither psychoanalysis nor eclectic psychotherapy, hynotherapy, client-centered psychotherapy, behavioral therapy, electroconvulsive therapy, or any other therapy made a significant difference in the increasing number of people who were forced by their bizarre behavior to spend months and years of their lives confined to a mental hospital.

Since 1955 the population of psychiatric hospitals relative to the general population has decreased every year. Why? The answer is very clear. In 1955 modern psychochemotherapy became widely available in the United States. Since its introduction, every year has seen a steady increase in the employment of psychochemotherapy.

Clearly, the use of psychochemicals has very much improved the old figure of two-thirds. Now patients who would have been dismissed as hopeless by psychotherapists are successfully treated, both by the use of psychotherapy with chemotherapy, and with the use of the behavioral reinforcements available to the patient in his everyday life. Today many a patient suffering from schizophrenia leads a relatively normal life after being discharged from the hospital, simply because he reports to a dispensing station once a month for a handful of medication which lasts until the next monthly visit. Between visits he is left to his own devices and often fares very well in his community where he is exposed to the usual behavioral rewards and punishments which exist in the world about him: family, friends, work, church, recreation.

The following case presentation illustrates an example of treatment for an emotionally disturbed patient by the use of behavior therapy (reprogramming) plus normalization of the patient (computer) through psychochemotherapy.

Norma J. was a twenty-four-year-old separated schoolteacher who presented herself to this therapist following nine months of unsuccessful psychotherapy with a "dynamically" (Freudian) oriented psychiatrist. Until a year previously, she was never aware of suffering from any emotional disturbance. Recently she had deserted her husband by eloping with another man. After living two weeks with her lover, she deserted him and returned home to live with her parents.

When interviewed by the therapist he found a restless, obviously depressed and distraught young woman who freely admitted that she had come to the end of her resources and could no longer continue to live unless her emotional life improved. She was oriented in significant spheres and was in good touch with reality. There was no evidence of bizarre ideation. Memory and recall were intact.

The past history revealed that this young lady had always made adequate grades both in high school and in college. Her life pattern had been one of acting out, passing from love affair to love affair, from party to party, always associated with considerable intake of alcohol from age fifteen. Recently she had graduated to marihuana, LSD, and speed.

It happened that the therapist was well acquainted with her family, having had two of her older sisters in therapy with him for anxiety reactions. The paternal grandfather was a grossly abnormal man who could best be described as a passive aggressive personality, who nevertheless managed to found and run a large industrial plant. The patient's father suffered from a severe obsessive-compulsive character disorder and had barely been able to hold onto his inherited business. The mother was a sensible woman with normal warmth and child rearing talents.

The early history revealed that this patient was unusual from the time of birth. She was a very quiet infant who preferred to be left alone. When picked up and fondled by her mother she screamed so loud that she was taken to a medical center for examination to make certain she had no spinal injury. As she grew older, she always stayed away from the other family members and would not allow herself to be fondled. She was described as shy until age fifteen, at which time she was said to suddenly lose her shyness and blossom forth into a charming person.

On the Wechsler Adult Intelligence Scale she scored 123 without any unusual spread in the subtest scores or between the verbal and performance scores. A Memory for Designs test was normal. The computer (Roche Psychiatric Service Institute) interpreted Minnesota Multiphasic Personality. Inventory comments are quoted, together with critical items which give the reader a clearer idea of her defense mechanisms and of the seriousness of her illness.

> The patient responded to the test items in a self-depreciating manner. At the present time her defenses are inadequate, and she is likely to focus on her failures and inability to cope with her problems.

This patient has a test pattern which is often associated with serious personality disorders. Medical patients with this pattern are characterized by vague physical complaints and considerable anxiety. Many appear to be early psychotic reactions, although they rarely show frankly bizarre behavior. Psychiatric patients with this pattern usually show more obviously deviant behavior. They are usually diagnosed as having a personality disorder or psychotic reaction. Usual manifestations are poor social adjustment, unusual or bizarre mentation or behavior, frequently in the sexual area.

In general, people with this test pattern are seen as odd or peculiar. It should be emphasized that the presence of this pattern is not conclusive evidence of a personality disorder. However, the high incidence of unusual behavior among patients with this pattern suggests that the patient should be carefully evaluated.

She is a rigid person who may respond to anxiety with phobias, compulsions or obsessive rumination. Chronic tension and excessive worry are common, and resistance to treatment may be extreme, despite the obvious distress.

She seems to be somewhat depressed at the present time. She is pessimistic about the future and distressed about real or imagined failures. Worry, discouragement and self-criticism may be expressed.

This person may be hesitant to become involved in social relationships. She is sensitive, reserved and somewhat uneasy, especially in new and unfamiliar situations. She may compensate by unusual conscientiousness in her work and other responsibilities.

This patient appears to be a resentful, constricted and embittered person. She is distrustful and apprehensive to a degree which interferes with her social interactions.

This patient has test features which resemble those of psychiatric outpatients who later required inpatient care. Continued professional care and observation are suggested.

The patient's test pattern resembles that of schizophrenics. The possibility of schizophrenia must be considered.

Critical Items

These test items, which were answered in the direction indicated, may require further investigation by the clinician. The clinician is cautioned, however, against overinterpretation of isolated responses.

168   There is something wrong with my mind. (TRUE)
182   I am afraid of losing my mind. (TRUE)
323   I have had very peculiar and strange experiences. (TRUE)
349   I have strange and peculiar thoughts. (TRUE)
 20   My sex life is satisfactory. (FALSE)
 37   I have never been in trouble because of my sex behavior. (FALSE)
133   I have never indulged in any unusual sex practices. (FALSE)
179   I am worried about sex matters. (TRUE)
302   I have never been in trouble because of my sex behavior. (FALSE)
146   I have the wanderlust and am never happy unless I am roaming or traveling about. (TRUE)
156   I have had periods in which I carried on activities without knowing later what I had been doing. (TRUE)
215   I have used alcohol excessively. (TRUE)
 44   Much of the time my head seems to hurt all over. (TRUE)
 85   Sometimes I am strongly attracted by the personal articles of others such as shoes, gloves, etc., so that I want to handle or steal them though I have no use for them. (TRUE)
114   I often feel as if there were a tight band about my head. (TRUE)
337   I feel anxiety about something or someone almost all the time. (TRUE)

An electroencephalogram was performed which was abnormal due to "some disorganization of the background and a mild paroxysmal quality."

We had the following evidence in favor of hardware damage: abnormal distanting and affective behavior from birth, strong family history of emotional difficulties, and abnormal electroencephalogram. "An abnormal EEG in an otherwise normal subject is strong evidence of an inborn constitutional abnormality involving the central nervous system." (Williams, 1941)

Because the patient had damaged hardware, it goes without saying that it was not possible for the programmer (mother) to program her Socially Programmed Computer in a normal manner. How is it possible to fully love (program) a child (computer) who will not allow herself to be fondled? How is it possible to keep from programming a negative Self-Concept into the SPC if the computer (child) is constantly intractable?

The abnormal hardware and lack of early normal programming of the Socially Programmed Computer (SPC) must of necessity influence all of Norma J.'s later social relationships.

But, from a therapeutic standpoint, it makes no difference whether this computer is abnormal because of defective hardware or because of a faulty Socially Programmed Computer or because of an abnormal Biologically Programmed Computer. The treatment is the same: normalization of the damaged hardware and software of the computer (with chemotherapy) followed by behavior therapy (reprogramming).

It will be recalled that Norma J. experienced a sudden flowering of her personality at age fifteen. Where she had been negativistic, quiet and withdrawn, she suddenly became outgoing and gay. Can this transformation be explained in terms of chemical and behavioral theory? A careful history revealed that this patient overcame her social inhibitions at the same time she began a rather heavy intake of alcohol and began dating. The two activities always coincided.

It is a common observation that the alcohol serves to reduce tension in intimate relationships. The alcohol had a chemical effect upon Norma J.'s nervous system (computer) which temporarily normalized it. While this effect lasted, Norma J. was free to establish intimacies. The sexual act constituted a means of reaching out, for the first time in her life, for a deep and much desired emotional relationship with another individual. Through process of trial and error, Norma J. was programmed to (1) drink alcohol, and (2) have sexual relations. The reason she was programmed to perform in this pattern was that, for the first time she was able to satisfy her need for close human contact, to reach a temporary homeostasis.

The history revealed that Norma J. never indulged in dating and sexual behavior unless she was at the same time taking a chemical (alcohol) which temporarily normalized a part of her computer so that it could act in a manner much like the other computers with whom she was surrounded. But we all know that it is hardly possible to stay in a constant state of alcoholicly induced "normality." The choice of alcohol as a normalizing chemical was unfortunate for several reasons:

1. Alcohol tends to break down the normal limitations placed upon behavior (short circuits the TOTEC for acting in our best interest in social situations) and thus patients tend to act in ways which are disintegrating. For example, while drinking she behaved sexually in ways which were unacceptable to the Self-Conception part of her SPC. By satisfying her BPC programs and her SPC programs in a manner unacceptable to the Self-Conception part of her SPC, she felt guilty, degraded, and finally, developed a depression.
2. Alcohol is a chemical with a physiological backlash which leaves the

computer sick (depression, nausea, headache, and all the other symptoms of what is commonly called "hangover").

3. The alcohol which at first normalized the computer, later caused complications for the computer. For example, by freeing her behavior of its usual programmed limitations, she left her husband, ran off with another man for whom she did not care, thus placing herself in a situation unacceptable both to her BPC and her SPC.

4. The alcohol acted, in effect, to enlarge her Skinner box in which she lived. Instead of being forced to experiment with discharging her BPC programs and SPC programs through socially acceptable institutions, she discharged these energies through play. Here we find a rat, symbolically speaking, who sat in a corner intoxicated and ignored the usual feeding needs and thus escaped being programmed in the usual manner.*

The whole life pattern of alcohol-social contact homeostasis finally broke down and she began to realize that she was not truly finding homeostasis, meeting her life's needs. Thus, through trial and error (TOTEC) she finally discovered that her whole life pattern was inappropriate. At this point of total defeat she consulted a dynamically oriented psychiatrist who treated her weekly over a nine-month period. Since he accepted her as basically a worthwhile person, he certainly attempted to reprogram the Self-Conception part of her Socially Programmed Computer.

But he failed in this reprogramming attempt because the patient (computer) continued her acting out behavior (sexual promiscuousness carried out during her continued alcoholic glow). Her Self-Conception, from long programming in early life, knew very well that such behavior was unacceptable. The therapist's acceptance alone was not strong enough reinforcement to significantly reprogram her SPC. Her Self-Conception remained punitive towards her, causing her to feel depressed and even helping her fail in therapy, since her Self-Conception felt she did not deserve anything more than unhappiness.

Also, her continued intake of alcohol prevented the therapist from reprogramming her activities into socially acceptable institutions. During this period she managed to work and keep house, but aside from these activities (and she was only marginally effective in these areas) she remained stationary.

---

* The author does not wish to imply that alcohol is disintegrating to all people. Many relatively intact people can use it in play (to temporarily escape their Skinner boxes). It is harmful to the young, who are in the process of being programmed, and to those persons with emotional problems of magnitude.

In no way did she find acceptable new ways for furthering her strong Expanding Programs. Haphazard sexual relations with many men was a perverted type of expression for her Expanding Programs, and led to nothing concrete. She did not increase her income or her prestige or even have any babies. Finally, as stated, in desperation she eloped with her husband's best friend. Two weeks later, when her new interest turned into boredom, she deserted this man, returned home, and presented herself to this therapist for help.

The tests mentioned earlier reflected her condition at the time she first presented herself for therapy. Because of the acute nature of her distress and because this therapist felt the patient was too ill to function well and respond to behavioral therapy alone, she was placed on psychochemotherapy in an attempt to normalize her computer so reprogramming could begin.

Whenever psychochemotherapy is begun, the therapist can only make an educated guess as to what medication or what combination of medications will be effective. With about eighty percent of the patients it is possible to prescribe the proper medication from the start, even though it may need to be adjusted from time to time. With the other twenty percent of the patients, the therapist must often go through a long period of trying several medications. In exceptional circumstances this therapist has changed medication for several years before finding the optimal combination of medications. Unfortunately, we do not yet have a sufficiently detailed knowledge of the chemistry of the central nervous system to scientifically arrive at an exact chemical diagnosis. Because each patient is so uniquely individual, only broad directions can be found from the literature on the subject of psychochemotherapy.

Norma J. was placed on chlordiazepoxide hydrochloride (10 mg. four times daily) and imipramine hydrochloride (10 mgs. three times daily). When she arrived for her second visit, the patient was markedly improved. She sat upright in the chair. Her face was lively and she had properly groomed herself. "What's really wrong with me?" she asked. "I don't know all the answers, but I think we will be able to work things out if you can give up alcohol," the therapist replied.

The therapist must develop a Master Plan for treating each patient. With Norma J. the plan was as follows:

1. To chemically normalize her computer.
2. To stop her alcohol intake, since the use of alcohol allowed her to stray out of her Skinner box and allowed her to behave in ways which were basically unacceptable to her Self-Concept.
3. To reprogram her (through the use of approval and the withholding of approval) so that she could find expressions of her Expanding Pro-

grams through social institutions which were acceptable to her Self-Concept.

4. To reprogram the Self-Conception part of her SPC.

"Giving up drinking and grass will be the easiest thing in the world," she stated, the stock answer such patients often give. They truly do not believe alcohol or drugs have anything to do with their illness. Later she began to talk about finding a job. The therapist showed a great deal of interest in this train of thought and so reinforced this activity (began reprogramming).

When the patient began work as a schoolteacher, her symptoms returned so that it was necessary to increase her chlordiazepoxide HCL to 20 mg. four times daily and her imipramine HCL to 20 mg. three times daily. Because of insomnia, in which she had dreams which were almost psychotic (too dramatic, filled with primary hostility involving clinical details of bloody injuries, etc.), it was decided to take away the bedtime chlordiazepoxide HCL and replace it with 50 mg. of Thioridazine HCL. The dreams subsided and she began sleeping well.

After a month she complained of extreme boredom. "What do people do after work if they don't go to a party and spend the evening drinking?" "You should be able to answer that question. You must know a few people who don't spend their evenings drinking."

With difficulty she was able to recall some people who spent their evening playing cards or taking night school courses or doing voluntary hospital work. "But all those people are dull. I wouldn't want to be like them." "You'd rather suffer the way you have been suffering?" "No, of course not." "Then you want to have your pie and eat it too." "Doesn't everyone?" "Yes, of course. But most people learn it's not possible." She laughed and changed to a less painful subject. A week later she had begun thinking about a night college course which would give her credit towards a master's degree. The therapist naturally reinforced this line of thought by showing interest.

But instead of applying for admission to the course, she went with a girl friend to a night club where she met a divorced fire extinguisher salesman. "You'd like him. He's so full of life." The therapist waited and watched for her to begin to break out of the Skinner box in which he had her confined. Several weeks later she returned quite depressed. "I feel like a whore on Sunday morning," she announced. "Would you like to tell me about it?" Of course she had started drinking and smoking marihuana and had been acting out sexually. On the previous Saturday night she had ended up in the fire extinguisher salesman's apartment. They were later joined by his roommate. The three of them spent the night in Expanding Programs which were not really acceptable to Norma J.'s Self-Conception. "So, what do you think of that?" she asked, after finishing her story. "I think you're trying to defeat therapy."

Thus the therapist gave a negative reinforcement to her activities which were not in her best interest, which were not acceptable to her Self-Conception and which helped her break out of the Skinner box where she was being programmed. "Did you use any birth control?" "No," she said, as if she knew that question would be next. "You do like to suffer, don't you?" "I guess so." "But it wouldn't have happened if you hadn't started drinking."

Most sick people, unless they take certain sensorium altering drugs, are kept within reasonable bounds of behavior (their Skinner box) by their inhibitions (SPC). "I must admit I like to drink. Life seems empty unless I have a drink or two." Soon the patient agreed to a further step in chemotherapy. She was placed on disulfirm, a medication which makes it impossible for the patient to take alcohol. With the addition of disulfirm, the drinking and sexual acting out behavior stopped. Now, approximately six months after beginning therapy, the transference neurosis was beginning.

Sophisticated rats who have had a taste of the good life of freedom, champagne, laughter, and orgies do not like to be confined to a Skinner box. "I dreamed about you last night," she soon announced rather coyly and waited for the therapist to ask her about the dream. In the dream she had been sitting in a restaurant eating spaghetti. Suddenly she happened to notice him and his friend at the next table. A waitress brought them a bottle of wine. They toasted one another and began drinking the wine. "What were your feelings?" "I was furious!" "Well," he said, to let her know that he could accept her anger toward him. "I guess you must feel that way about me sometimes now that I give you medication to help you control your drinking." "That's exactly how I feel." "Pretty natural, wouldn't you say?" "I suppose so. I really don't know why I pay you good money to torture me this way." "Don't you know why?" "Of course I do. You're trying to help me. It's for my own good. But that only makes it more frustrating because I don't really know who to be angry at." "Life." "Yes, I guess so." "You'll have to remember I didn't make the world this way. But it's only natural you should want to blame me sometimes."

The boredom returned. This time, in seeking homeostasis, she signed up for an evening college course rather than starting out on her old road of alcohol and orgies. Because she now suffered from an increase in anxiety (confined in the rather small Skinner box), it was necessary to add Diphenyl-hydantoin (75 mgs. three times daily) to her medication. Excellent symptomatic

relief followed this maneuver. Her computer (hardware) was further normalized and reprogramming proceeded more rapidly.

The patient has now been in therapy for a little over three years. She
continued to work and progressed toward her master's degree. In addition,
she went to the YWCA two nights a week to practice with a swimming team.
Thus she was being reprogrammed to express her Expanding Programs
through socially acceptable institutions. She was (once her computer was
chemically normalized) reprogrammed both through her contact with her
therapist and through her contacts with other people, so that the Self-
Conception compartment of her Socially Programmed Computer became
more accepting of her and no longer punitive.

The patient complained of being unable to fall in love with her boy friend.
At last she left him, moved to another city and began teaching there. With this
radical change in her life she began to suffer from considerable anxiety and
developed phobic symptoms once more. It was at about this point that the
author began trying the megavitamin psychochemotherapy of Hoffer and
Osmond. With the addition of niacinamide, her symptoms rapidly came
under control and it was possible to cut her other medication by half. Since
the addition of megavitamin therapy, the quality of her improvement has
been remarkable. For the first time in her life she has been able to be close
to another person without the barrier melting (but personality shattering) use
of alcohol. She has broken with her old boy friend and is about to marry
another man who is clearly more suitable for her.

Reviewing the case, it is now clear to the author that this patient was
suffering from what could best be described as alcoholic schizophrenia.
Undoubtedly it would have been best to use megavitamin therapy from the
beginning; however, the author did not become aware of its usefulness until
recently.

Each time we lower her medication, she begins to develop so great an
anxiety that it threatens her with disintegration. Possibly she will require
psychochemotherapy indefinitely. But even so, the medication has allowed
her to expand her life in ways that would never have been possible otherwise.
Even if she must continue the medication, she is in no worse position than a
patient with diabetes who must take insulin all her life.

We cure very few disorders in the world of medicine. In psychiatry, as in
other fields of medical endeavor, we are often only able to help the patient to
better utilize a biologically damaged organ. We can often control hypertension, diabetes, arthritis, heart diseases, and other disorders, though we
seldom cure them.

CHAPTER 17

Therapy in Relation to Age of Patient

All forms of therapy for emotional disorders are altered to fit the particular needs of the patient's age group. With Neo-Behavioral Psycho-chemotherapy the needs for different age groups can be very logically determined.

In every group of animals living in a social relationship, the young are placed in a programming situation in order that they may be programmed to fit into the social structure in which they spend their adult years. At first the mother is the child's programmer, followed by the father, other siblings, relatives, school and then the world at large.

In treating the child (reprogramming him) the therapist makes the fullest use of the programmers which surround the child. Thus the therapist spends much of his time helping parents and teachers set up a proper Skinner box with proper rewards in which to program the child effectively.

For example, this therapist was asked to see a five-year-old boy because he cried, kicked, and refused to leave the car to enter kindergarten. A history revealed that the grandparents lived in the home with the mother, father, and child. The grandfather, a man who had always been frustrated in his attempts at developing satisfying personal relationships, had "adopted" the child. He would take the child on numerous automobile excursions, buy him any toy requested, and would oppose the parents whenever they attempted to discipline the child.

Clearly this child was not being programmed correctly. Instead of having the child in a Skinner box where he would behave (press the bar) in acceptable ways for acceptable rewards (love, approval) the child was given everything he desired simply by being himself.

The child's Expanding Programs were quite strong, like those of his father and grandfather. In the home, the child was master. His Expanding Programs were easily met. In the schoolroom, on the other hand, he was only another child, was not able to control the people there. Naturally the child achieved satisfaction (homeostasis) for his Expanding Programs best by remaining at home rather than going to school.

The therapist advised the parents to circumvent the grandfather, to physically carry the child into the schoolroom and leave him there regardless of his pleas. The grandfather resisted this advice so strongly that it was necessary for the father and mother to move with their child into another house. The father carried the child to school, deposited him kicking and screaming in the classroom and left the building.

The child made a valiant effort to regain his lost Expanding Program by screaming, refusing to eat and pouting for several days, but at the end of the week he was opening the car door and entering the school unassisted. After another week, he had given up his fight as a lost cause. School (programming) progressed in the normal manner. Here we see an example of a therapist reprogramming the child largely through the use of the normal programming situation which already surrounded the child.

Whenever a child or teenager develops significant emotional problems, biological damage is likely to be prominent. He may have damaged hardware. For example, he may have sustained minimal brain damage due to anoxemia at birth, may have had a mild case of measles encephalitis or be suffering from early schizophrenia. The child could have an abnormal Biologically Programmed Computer (BPC). That is to say he may have unusually strong Expanding Programs or he may be very intractable. For this reason very likely psychochemotherapy will be needed rather than a mere change in his environment to facilitate reprogramming or reprogramming with psycho-therapy.

Last year this therapist was consulted by a family with a nine-year-old boy who was making poor marks in school. He was negativistic, hyperactive, distractible, and seemed to be on the point of seriously injuring his younger brother. This child had been seen by one therapist who advised the parents to be more strict with the boy. When this did not work, they consulted a second therapist who advised them to be more lenient with him. This maneuver brought no results.

Psychological tests (WAIS) showed the child to have normal intelligence, but a 17-point spread between the verbal and performance I.Q. His electro-encephalogram was slightly abnormal. A diagnosis of minimal brain dysfunction was made and the boy was placed on Deanol Acetamidobenzoate

300 mg. daily, Niacinamide 1500 mg. daily, Ascorbic acid 1500 mg. daily and pyridoxine 150 mg. daily. The only change made in his Skinner box was to advise the parents to let the boy give up piano lessons and to encourage his participation in sports. Certainly school work used up all this child's ability to concentrate. The piano lessons were entirely inappropriate. He began playing football as an outlet for his strong physical Expanding Programs.

After making these changes in the environment and placing the boy on psychochemotherapy, his life rapidly settled into a normal pattern. He is now tractable and pleasant, making much better marks in school, and no longer physically abuses his little brother. He returns for a thirty minute visit every three months. Whenever his medication is reduced, many of his symptoms return. He will be maintained on medication for at least another year or two at which time a trial reduction will be made.

Here we see quite clearly the importance of using psychochemotherapy for a child. After normalizing his computer with psychochemistry the normal programming situation surrounding him (parents and school) could begin programming him in the normal manner. There would have been no point in having the child spend long, expensive hours with the therapist. He was suffering from a minimal brain damage (damaged hardware) which could be normalized with psychochemotherapy, leaving him free to be programmed correctly by his usual programmers.

It is with the patient from age, roughly, eighteen to thirty-five, where behavioral psychotherapy requires the patient to have the most contact with the therapist. During these years, the patient is not living in as small a Skinner box, nor does he have so many programmers in his life, as during the early years when he was a child and still surrounded by family and school.

Lacking the parent and the school as programmers, the young adult has much more need for an intimate relationship with a therapist who can proceed with the reprogramming, with or without the aid of psychochemistry, depending largely upon the depth of disturbance the patient is experiencing. Norma J.'s therapy was described earlier and illustrates the type of therapy often required by the young adult.

Older people have already received most of their programming. A forty-year-old postman is not likely to be reprogrammed so that further realization of his Expanding Drives leads him into becoming a surgeon and be granted a Nobel prize.

The author has in mind a patient, age forty-seven, who is currently in therapy. This man has had intermittent emotional troubles all through his life, but has never received anything other than first aid. Not long ago he presented himself at the office. He was depressed and agitated to the point he missed going to work at least half the time. A man of extraordinary fortitude, he still made an effort to carry on with his duties in spite of a depression of near psychotic proportions.

Here the therapist was presented with a psychiatric emergency: a middle-aged man is about to lose his ability to work. Even if prolonged reprogramming (psychotherapy) were possible, it would not be effective soon enough to save the structure of this man's life. During the first session the patient's valiant attempts at continuing work were reinforced. "You've been working under a tremendous handicap," he was told. "And I think you deserve a great deal of credit for not giving up." Here he was being programmed to continue his struggle to work and a first step was made toward reprogramming him for a more favorable Self-Concept.

It was not possible to make an exact diagnosis as to whether this man had damaged hardware or software. Such a diagnosis is not necessary since behavioral therapy plus psychochemotherapy is effective for almost all seriously ill patients. Clearly with a man so ill, more than reprogramming was required. He was placed on Thioridazine (50 mgs. four times daily), Amitriptyline (25 mgs. four times daily), and Amobarbital (200 mgs. at bedtime). Soon this medication was changed to Thioridazine (100 mgs. four times daily), Desipramine (50 mgs. four times daily), and the Amobarbital was continued. When he developed extra pyramidal signs, Benztropine Mesylate (1 mg. four times daily) was added. Then the patient began to lose his memory. The Benztropine mesylate was reduced (to 1 mg. two times daily), and the other medication continued at the former level. Very soon the patient was working every day and beginning to come out of his depression.

Not long after this, the patient received a serious injury in an automobile accident, such that it was necessary for him to remain at home for several months. During this period his depression and anxiety returned in spite of continued medication. At this point an HOD test showed perceptual defects. Only when niacin (1000 mgs. three times daily) and ascorbic acid (1000 mgs. three times daily) were added to his medication did he improve again. Soon it was possible to halve his other medication.

Rather than reprogramming this man for new activities, his present level of work will simply be reinforced. Only his Self-Conception will be greatly altered by reprogramming techniques. How long will he require psycho-chemotherapy? Quite possibly for the rest of his life.

CHAPTER 18

The Reinforcement of Negative Behavior

Parent, teacher, relative, husband, wife, government, or therapist may find themselves, as programmers, reinforcing negative behavior. Since this is such a serious mistake for anyone engaged in programming, it seems appropriate to point out several examples in order that this mistake can be avoided.

Several weeks ago in this community a teenage boy took LSD and decided he needed to see his girl friend at once. When he telephoned her at two thirty in the morning she told him her family would never allow her to leave the house at such an hour. After being refused, the boy went over to her house and rang the front doorbell. The girl's father answered the door and told the boy to go away, that he was not being sensible. When the father closed the door, the boy went back to his automobile where he found a jack, with which he proceeded to break down the front door and enter the house. While this was occurring the father telephoned the police who arrived and carried the boy off to jail.

This was not the first time this seventeen-year-old boy had been in trouble. Nevertheless, the boy's father was able to handle the whole matter out of court. But by helping the boy avoid an unpleasant court appearance and judicial action, the father was failing to let the boy have an experience which would have been a negative reinforcement for his behavior.

To make matters all the worse, the father, following this boy's unfortunate behavior, bought the boy an automobile. "This has been such a trying experience for the boy, I bought him a car to help him forget all the trouble," the father explained. The reader will certainly see that the father was positively reinforcing his son's unacceptable behavior, encouraging him to break down doors and perform other antisocial acts. Here we clearly see a parent programming a child to act in an antisocial manner.

The next example shows a college dean reinforcing negative behavior. A nineteen-year-old girl at a college fell in love with a boy from a distant State. She began flying over to see the boy every few weekends. Her father told her she was to stop this activity, that, in the first place, she would never catch a boy by running after him, that it cost too much money to make these trips, and that she left on Friday and returned on Monday afternoon, making her miss time in the classroom. Her grades were falling. The father had sent her to college at considerable expense to get an education. If she did not value an education she should stop college and go to work.

The young lady consulted the Dean of Women about the problem. The Dean told her: "You're a grown person and it's time for you to make your own decisions. Go ahead and see your boy friend. Your father won't cut off your allowance as he threatened to do." Thus the Dean was reinforcing the girl's negative behavior.

Recently, an intoxicated middle-aged woman was brought to the office for a consultation by her grown daughter. The woman had a bruised cheek, and several of her teeth were missing. She sat in the corner and mumbled to herself while the daughter gave the history. Her mother had been hospitalized twice in recent months for alcoholism. In spite of everything the family could do, they had not been able to keep her sober. Quite obviously the woman was in no shape for outpatient treatment.

"Are you really interested in curing your mother?" the therapist asked. He was assured that the daughter wanted to do everything possible to help her mother.

The young lady was advised to rehospitalize her mother every time she took even a small drink. "But Mother doesn't like the hospital," the daughter protested. "Good." "You want to punish her for getting drunk? That doesn't sound like very good treatment." "I don't want to punish your mother. I only want to present her with two choices: she may drink and go to live in the hospital, or she may remain sober and stay at home. The choice is her own: hospital or home."

In this manner the patient would receive behavioral therapy. Acceptable behavior would be reinforced (programmed) and unacceptable behavior would receive negative reinforcement. "You don't have a very good bedside manner," the mother muttered as she left the office!

It would have been possible for the therapist to see this woman several times a week for years without bringing about any change in her behavior. By putting her in a proper Skinner box where she could make a choice, there was a good chance of helping this woman. As a matter of fact the woman did return and, except for one additional hospitalization following an attempt to test her daughter and the therapist, she has been sober for more than two years.

Therapists frequently reinforce unacceptable behavior. Recently a teen-ager visited the author's office after being discharged from one of the country's leading luxury psychiatric hospitals. The boy was still suffering from schizophrenia and was quite upset while an effort was being made to get him regulated on a proper combination of psychochemotherapy. "I want to go back to the hospital. Life's too difficult on the outside," he announced. His mother was called in and told that she should let her son know that if he were hospitalized again, he would have to go to a state hospital, rather than back to his loving therapist at the luxury hospital where all kinds of ridiculous behavior was condoned.

On his next visit to the office the boy complained at length to the therapist that he was not fond of him and did not care what happened to him. "I like the healthy part of you and feel you have great potential as a person," he was told, "but I dislike the unhealthy part of you. I'm going to do everything possible to get rid of your unhealthy side."

Later he complained that to be confined to a state hospital was beneath him socially, that he understood patients in state hospitals had to scrub floors, help feed patients, and do all kinds of menial work. After giving the boy a choice of state hospital or struggling with his problems, he made a choice: he would keep struggling. Now he is attending college and doing very well. He owes his success not only to psychochemotherapy but also to behavior therapy. Unlike his hospital psychiatrist, who would approve of him regardless of his behavior, his present therapist would give approval only when it was earned.

We live in an age in which freedom and love (under the label of humanism) are the key ideas. This is an outgrowth of man's long attempt to climb out of the constriction of the Middle Ages and reach a new plateau of happiness. Unfortunately, neither are young people being programmed for life, nor can emotionally disturbed persons be programmed or reprogrammed in an atmosphere of freedom and love. They can only be programmed or repro-grammed if placed in a Skinner box and given love only when they perform in a manner which will allow them to grow into more complete persons, when they express their Biological and Social Programs through proper social institutions.

PART III

Social Implications

CHAPTER 19

Anger and Aggression

First a definition of terms is given to clarify the following discussion.

By *anger* is meant all the friction which results from frustration of the programs of man's Biologically Programmed Computer as well as the fustrations which result from the frustrations of his Socially Programmed Computer. In short, whatever interferes with any need produces anger. The term anger is used to cover every negative feeling from vexation to frank rage.

By *aggression* is meant the act of taking—the Expanding Programs of the Biologically Programmed Computer. If Hitler takes Austria, this is an act of aggression. If Farmer Brown shoots a squirrel to eat, this is an act of aggression. If Mrs. Brown plays bingo at the church social in an attempt to win a prize, or if she sells eggs collected from her chickens, this is an act of aggression. If Sam X. rapes Mrs. Brown, this is an act of aggression on Sam X's part, unless Mrs. Brown enticed him to rape her, in which case Mrs. Brown would commit the act of aggression.

Clearly, aggression (Expanding Programs) may be either constructive (discharged in a manner which benefits mankind) or destructive (harms mankind).

The human is somewhat unique among living creatures partly because:

1. His Biologically Programmed Computer contains Expanding Programs (aggressions) which are far stronger than those of any other being. Man is the sexiest, the most ambitious, the most restless, the cleverest, the most easily bored, the most ruthless, the most energetic primate living. For between one and two million years he has been a meat eater, which means he was selectively bred (Biologically Programmed) to kill, to eat at the expense of other animals. He can now kill anything, including the world in which he lives.

2. Because of his protracted childhood, man's Socially Programmed Computer is programmed for a longer period of time than any other living creature. This is necessary to help him hold in check the powerful programs of his Biologically Programmed Computer. Man ends up with not only the world's most powerful Biologically Programmed Computer, but also with the world's most powerful Socially Programmed Computer. During the prolonged years of dependency man is bound (programmed) with ropes of love to his mother, his father, his siblings, and to mankind in general. These social bonds (programming of the SPC) begin at an early age and go on for many years. Man's dependency needs are never put aside. Even as an adult, he is dependent upon the goodwill of his fellow men; dependent upon the farmer to feed him, the clothing manufacturer to clothe him, and the policeman to protect him. He is dependent upon his mate for love and sexual satisfaction, upon his church for spiritual comfort and to allow him to feel he still lives securely within a family structure, upon his lodge members for fellowship, and upon his company for the money needed to pay other men to fulfill many needs.

Now it is clear that the Biologically Programmed Computer (BPC) and the Socially Programmed Computer (SPC) are in direct conflict with one another. The result can only be frustration, anger. *Man, having the strongest BPC and the strongest SPC, ends up by being the angriest creature on earth.* If he fulfills the programs of his BPC, he frustrates the programs of his SPC. If he satisfies the programs for his SPC, he frustrates the programs for his BPC.

For example, an insurance salesman belongs to a service club. Why did he join the club? He joined to fulfill the programs of the Socially Programmed Computer, so that he may find fellowship (love), so that he may serve his fellow man through the good works the club will perform, so that he can make his Self-Conception more acceptable. But he also joined the club so the Expanding Programs of his Biologically Programmed Computer can be fulfilled. For example, by joining the club, he forms a brotherhood with the other powerful members of his community. They will help protect him if he gets into difficulty. They will send business his way. Membership in the club will give him more prestige, so that he will more easily advance his business company, give his wife a higher station, help his sons find better jobs and his daughters find better husbands. Finally, he joined the club because his Test-Operate Test-Exit Computer told him that to join the club was the best way (best compromise) for achieving homeostasis, for serving both his SPC programs and his BPC programs without getting himself into difficulty.

But joining the club is a compromise which, in reality, totally satisfies neither his SPC programs nor his BPC programs. If the insurance salesman satisfied his BPC as it would like to be satisfied, he would walk into the club meeting and slay all the other insurance salesmen so they would not give him competition. He would be the only insurance salesman left, so the community would be forced to buy all its insurance through him. After slaying the other insurance salesmen, he would visit their homes and promptly impregnate all their wives, thus further satisfying his Expanding Programs. Afterwards, he would take what money they had left, as well as any objects which happened to catch his eyes: a camera, a pair of gold cuff links and a Grant Wood original. Then he would put his new "wives" and "children" to work for him. The wives would go out and sell insurance under his name. The children would shine his shoes, wash his automobile, and perform various other functions. Here we see a man who is satisfying the programs of his Biologically Programmed Computer.

But if he acted in such an antisocial manner, the programs of his Socially Programmed Computer would be totally frustrated. He would be cut off from the fellowship (love) which he desired. His Self-Image would be blackened beyond repair. He would not get the pleasure of helping his community through the good works of the club. What, on the other hand, would happen if the insurance salesman joined the club and served only the programs of his Socially Programmed Computer?

If the insurance salesman joined the club and tried to satisfy only his SPC programs, he would spend all of his waking hours helping his fellow clubmen. If one of his fellow club members had a heart attack, the insurance salesman would go to his store and give a hand to help keep the man's business afloat. He would visit the man in the hospital, help him with bills, invite the man's family to live at his house and share his table.

The insurance salesman satisfying only his SPC programs would spend any time left in his day helping the club sell brooms to benefit the Crippled Children's Clinic which the club supported, and in general demonstrating the love he felt for his fellow man. Thus he would satisfy his SPC programs, but his BPC programs would be completely unsatisfied. He would lose his own business, be unable to buy food for his mate and children, fail to reach homeostasis even though he did satisfy his SPC programs. Since he would not fulfill his BPC programs, the salesman would still end up frustrated, angry. Thus, no matter how the insurance salesman acts in relationship to his club, he will, in the end, feel a certain lack of satisfaction, a definite lack of homeostasis—anger.

Because man has such powerful programs both for his SPC and his BPC, it is his fate to forever live in a state of anger. This anger is not the anger of an ant or a mouse—it is the anger of a creature who has the power to kill everything, to kill not only his fellow club members, but to kill his whole community, to destroy the entire earth.

Mankind's anger is so powerful, so all pervasive, so permanent, that he is constantly in danger of being destroyed by this anger. Mankind has such a load of undischargeable anger and aggression that he is constantly threatened with annihilation by the results of the very forces which saved him from the sabertoothed tiger and the ice ages. To understand the destructive force of mankind's anger better, perhaps it should be discussed at this point in further detail.

When speaking of the insurance salesman's anger, I do not mean that there is danger of his pulling a rifle from his car in the town square at high noon and shooting a dozen of his fellow men. Neither do I mean that he somehow works his way into the intercontinental ballistic missile control center in Omaha and starts an atomic war. Rather this frustrated (angry) man carries his anger with him from day to day, much as he might carry an un-exploded cartridge in his pocket. To look at him you would never guess that he carries this unexploded charge of anger in his pocket.

How will this hidden anger, which we speak of as being so dangerous, show itself? Perhaps when the insurance salesman returns home at night he will switch on his TV set to a comedy show and see someone slapped in the face with a cream pie. The insurance salesman will laugh. He is having a discharge for his anger. Later our man may pick up the evening paper and read about the coed murders in Michigan. The editor ran the article in the newspaper because he knew people would be interested in the murders and would buy his paper to read about them. The insurance salesman enjoys reading about the murders because reading about another man's acts of anger helps him discharge some of his stored anger. On the late movie he might watch a cowboy track down a bad man and have an anger satisfying shoot-out, good old-fashioned naked killing. But still the insurance man's anger is of no real threat to humanity. The illustrations given show him dis-charging his anger in socially innocuous ways.

What happens in the political arena? A politician who advocates, for example, that we bomb China to extinction before she has a chance to attack us, may appeal to this angry insurance salesman. If there are enough angry men they will vote in an angry leader, thus giving power to an angry man who may be placed in a position to harm mankind.

More important, perhaps, is the harm done by a leader who waxes aggressive and angry after he has reached office, a man who does all the wrong things seemingly for the right reason. He may sometimes be backed (as reflected in opinion polls) by a host of angry citizens and thus encouraged to pursue his plans.

History is crowded with angry, aggressive leaders who kill for what they convince their followers is a "right" reason: Napoleon, Hitler, Castro. It is always possible to find a "right" reason for killing. If you separate two grammar school children who are fighting in the playground you will discover each of them has a "right" reason for fighting. The danger to mankind is that someday one of these angry, aggressive, "right" leaders will be backed by a great number of aggressive, angry, "right" citizens, and they will find a "right" reason to employ atomic, chemical, and bacteriological warfare, and in the course of their "right" war wipe out humanity.

What is the history of mankind's anger and aggression? For three reasons prehistoric man's anger and aggression surely must not have posed the problem it now poses for modern man.

Firstly, Stone Age man lived in tribal units of about 30 people. This meant that all of his behavior was readily observable and controllable by all the members of his tribe. The individual needed his tribe not only for social reasons, but also because his very survival depended upon his acceptance by the other members of the tribe. If a man was expelled from the tribe, no other tribe would take him in. He would be left to suffer alone on his own devices. If he did not die of loneliness, he would die of starvation or exposure. He could not even effectively hunt his meat without the cooperation of the other tribal members. This absolute dependency upon the other people of his tribe meant that he was compelled to cooperate with them and be very careful how he opposed either their social structures or their personalities. *Thus early man lived in a very structured environment, in a very small Skinner box where he could be readily programmed. Indeed to survive, he was forced to submit to intensive programming.*

In the *second* place, prehistoric mankind's anger and aggression were readily discharged by the primary conflicts for survival in his everyday life. When a dozen primitive men left the cave in the morning to search for meat, they had a day's work on their hands. They had to track down the bear, drive him to his death over a cliff or attack him in unison with stone-pointed spears. The actual killing of the bear would give great primary satisfaction to their BPC and would be a ready means of discharging anger and aggression. Not only was primitive man in conflict with his prey, but he was also in conflict with nature. He had to struggle through rain and snow to hunt.

The *third* reason primitive man's anger and aggression were not as bothersome to him as modern man's was because he was relatively weak, both in terms of firepower and in terms of wealth. Lacking the convenient weapons for slaying his fellow man, he was less likely to attack him. Even if he did attack his fellow man, his chances of slaying him, rather than merely injuring him, were slight. Of course wealth is required to effect any large scale attack such as war. For primitive man wealth consisted primarily of food. A people without a stored supply of food is in no position to wage war. If a people is preoccupied with feeding problems, that problem must take precedent over all others.

Biologically man has not changed for about thirty-five thousand years, but, between five and ten thousand years ago, he experienced a radical change in his whole pattern of living. After this change, anger and aggression, rather than food gathering, became his primary problem. It was during this period that man became an agricultural animal. Specifically, he began raising grain and started practicing animal husbandry. His primary caloric intake of food shifted from meat to grain, which could be stored. This constituted the first wealth and allowed man to live in large groups for the first time. Thus we find the first cities; and with their advent, man's anger and aggression began to come to the forefront of his problems, pushing aside his problem of food gathering.

With the advent of the city, profound changes took place.

1. Man replaced the tribal unit (with its fixed personal social structure) with the city unit (with its relatively impersonal, unstable social structure). This meant that he no longer lived in a small Skinner box where he could be readily programmed. He no longer depended for survival directly upon the goodwill of each man who touched his life.
2. The city man no longer had a direct primary outlet for his anger and aggression. He no longer struggled with nature and personally killed his food.
3. Because of the wealth of his granaries, man could afford war. Also his weapons became more powerful, sophisticated and mobile.

The move to the cities progressed in ancient times until it culminated in the Roman Empire. Here was man with all his new, and relatively weak social institutions, with his undreamed of wealth, and with such an alienation from primary discharges for his anger and aggression that he staged circuses in order to release his killing programs secondhand. But Roman civilization eventually began to disintegrate. War, sexual degeneracy, man killing man in the arena must finally have sickened man to the point where he realized some other form of social structure was necessary, if he were to be prevented from destroying himself with the programs of his BPC and his anger.

The author would like to make it clear that he does not oppose Christianity, or any other religion. If man did follow the teachings of Christ, he would surely be in a better position than that which he finds himself in today. However, a large segment of the public does not follow these teachings. Religion, realistically speaking, has not solved mankind's problems. The yearly crime statistics published by J. Edgar Hoover would lead one to believe that Billy Graham is losing his crusade. The author doubts that the bulk of mankind is, in its present state of biological and scientific development, capable of following Christianity.

At the point where Roman civilization began to disintegrate, Christianity began to enfold the Western World. This was an attempt by man to deny the programs of his Biologically Programmed Computer and to deny his anger. Also Christianity tightened the social structure, and once more placed man in a small Skinner box where he could readily be programmed through the promise of Heaven and the threat of Hell. Christianity was relatively effective in controlling man's anger and his BPC programs. These controls produced the rigid, rather stereotyped society of the Middle Ages.

But man, as a part of his Expanding Programs (aggression), always tries to free himself from his Skinner box, hence he is continually in conflict with the social institutions which surround him. An artist is motivated to paint in a style different from that of his teachers. A teacher tries to use new methods which are different from those of the preceding generation. A historian wants to interpret history in a different light. A minister wishes to present the Scriptures in a new way. A musician, a politician, a dress designer, a physician; everyone is motivated by his BPC to overthrow the Establishment (the social institutions which are part of his Skinner box).

Since the Church formed such an important part of mankind's Skinner box during the Middle Ages, it was only natural that men should seek to overthrow it. In about 1457 Gutenberg's press came into use. This invention was of great significance in man's attempt to break out of the Middle Ages' Skinner box. Science soon began its attack on the divine origin of man, and, of necessity, upon the Church itself.

Copernicus, a canon of the cathedral of Frauenburg, discovered that the earth was merely one of several planets which revolved around the sun. Wisely, for his own good health, he did not allow his findings to be published until he lay on his death bed. In spite of his having dedicated the volume to Pope Paul III, the Church reacted violently against this new conception of the universe, which, in its eyes, attempted to take away the dignity of man.

More than a century later when Galileo confirmed the findings of Copernicus, he was imprisoned by the Church and forced to renounce his endorsement. Rightly the Church considered the new theory about the universe as a direct attack upon its authority, as a vigorous attempt on the part of mankind to break out of the Skinner box in which it was confined.

This erosion of man's divine nature continued, and received the severest jolt during the 19th century when Darwin demonstrated that man was only another animal which had evolved from a "lower" form of life. Understandably, again, the Church fought this erosion of its establishment.

In the 20th century Freud gave mankind a further blow, took away yet another layer of its divinity, this one psychological. Again, the Church opposed Freud. Now, during the second half of the 20th century, Skinner's instrumental behavioral psychology and the discoveries regarding the chemistry of the central nervous system have dealt more blows to the Establishment.

Science is still opposed because it keeps eroding the Skinner box. The Church today has lost much of its power over a large segment of the Western World. It no longer effectively acts as a programmer for most people. Science, having robbed mankind of his most powerful social institutions (first the tribe, and then the Church) has left man in a state of relative chaos, without a strong, small Skinner box in which to become programmed.

Mankind, following its Expanding Programs, has continued to attack its social institutions, all the institutions which have, in the past, acted as its Skinner box. With the ever increasing expansion of science and the ever increasing efficiency of communications, man finds his family life, his former ideas of government, his conception of class stratification, his traditional role of university, all threatened, weakened by his attacks. The very conceptions of honor, personal integrity and pride are being dissolved.

Some members of society are attempting to correct the confusion, the symptoms of decay, in which the world finds itself. Men who consider themselves, "radical, advanced, enlightened, progressive" are striving to correct the poverty, the illegitimacy, the unemployment, the crime, the mental illness—the unhappiness which engulfs mankind.

In reality these "progressive men" only further tear away at the social structure, incorrectly concluding that mankind will somehow be magically saved if everyone can be free, if everyone is given a minimum income, if everyone is equal. Billions of dollars are spent by governments in vain attempts to correct the social pathology which pervades much of the world. Quite obviously one need only read a daily paper to see that the objectives are not being reached.

It would seem reasonable to conclude that man's social ills can only be altered by changing the programming of his Socially Programmed Computer or by biologically altering his Biologically Programmed Computer. It would be possible to change man's SPC by changing his social structure so that he was once more placed in a small Skinner box where he could be efficiently programmed.

Strong social institutions, such as the Church during the Middle Ages, could be reinstated. This has been attempted, but it has not, and it is suspected, will not succeed. We have seen, during the 20th century, the formation of a new religion, Marxism, which has put its followers in a small Skinner box where they could be efficiently programmed.

This new religion, based on pseudo-science, was begun by Marx and put into action by Lenin. However, it was not until Stalin reached power and created the dreaded All-Russia Extraordinary Commission for Combating Counterrevolution, Sabotage, and Speculation, under Dzerzhinsky, that the whole Russian people were plunged into a very tight Skinner box

They were given a goal (Master Plan) to work toward: achievement of material benefits here on earth and the establishment of the first Communist state where everyone would be equal. They were reinforced (programmed) with approval, with food and housing when they worked toward this goal. If they failed to work toward it, if they did not support it, the secret police headed up by Dzerzhinsky had them eliminated. Thus a great nation was very effectively programmed.

The effect upon social pathology was prompt and spectacular. Crime, prostitution, juvenile delinquency, unemployment, and illegitimate pregnancies were greatly reduced. At first, family life was adversely affected because divorce was made easy by a new government policy. The policy was soon reversed, however, when it became clear that a strong family unit was necessary for the very early programming of the child. Great stress was put on education because the school and university were recognized as holding a very important position in the programming of the younger generation.

Today, Soviet social structure is beginning to loosen. The religion of Marxism is starting to disintegrate, not because its members have eroded its structure through the medium of science, but because the Expanding Programs of the citizen's Biologically Programmed Computer has motivated him to break out of his small Skinner box.

Each regime since Stalin, with a few minor oscillations, has been more liberal than its predecessor. The younger generation, in spite of intense programming, wants to paint in an unapproved "decadent" abstract style, wishes to criticize the government through the medium of literature, and takes great pleasure in the "decadent" music which Stalin forbade. In the field of economics, as another example, the new generation has instituted monetary incentive rewards for increased factory production, has allowed individual industries much more autonomy in production and distribution of its goods. Every man is not paid the same wage and does not live on the same scale in the Soviet Union. Government officials have taken their place as an elite social caste with special housing and transportation privileges and special considerations for their children.

With this erosion of the rigid religious institutions of Marxism has come a return of the various forms of social pathology which had been under very good control a generation before. In another generation or two it will, in all probability, be difficult to distinguish Soviet Russia from the Western nations. Their tight Skinner box will have been destroyed and their people will no longer be intensely programmed.

If a governmental agency was established to engineer our society through behavioral techniques, people would peck away at the agency (social structure) until its original purposes was undermined, and it finally collapsed.

The author has attempted to illustrate his theory that, modern science, communication, and wealth being what it is, it is not possible for man to solve his social problems by revising his social institutions. Even if he does solve his problems in this manner, the institutions will rapidly erode and he will be right back with the problems of social disintegration in his lap again.

Thus present day "liberals" who maintain that man's problems can be solved with "social reforms" are, in reality, very old fashioned. They are still vainly trying to plug holes in an old dike with their fingers. They honestly believe that all they need is more fingers to solve the problem. This social approach to the solution of social problems fails because it does not take into account one of man's basic biological structures, i.e., his Biologically Programmed Computer which has powerful Expanding Programs, and which includes killing and destruction.

Perhaps only one change could be made in our social structure which would solve our social programs: the return to a Stone Age life where people lived in tribal groups of thirty and hunted down their food every day. Since the human population of the world is too great for tribal living, and the game too scarce; since mankind is not likely to enact a return to tribal life; and since man would not remain in a tribal situation even if he were placed there, perhaps he should look to the science of biology for the solutions to his social, and, ultimately, his emotional problems. *It might be wise for man to stop concentrating on his Socially Programmed Computer and turn his attention to his Biologically Programmed Computer.*

It would seem that if man is ever to solve his social problems he must first accept the fact that he is a biological creature and that, in the end, all behavior and social problems are rooted in his biology.

Marriage, for example, is a social institution, but its feet stand in the clay of biology. Its most obvious biological connection is with the Expanding Programs of the Biologically Programmed Computer commonly known as sex. But the roots of the social institution called marriage spread far beyond sex. The institution of marriage itself is thought by many to have originated as an aid to solving primitive man's food gathering techniques. When man lived in common with as many wives as he could control, he had to constantly defend them against poachers. This hindered him in his food gathering activities. Later, when man settled in more or less fixed abodes, he had to leave home to hunt down food. This meant his wives were left unprotected from any member of the tribe who chose to double back to his home and enjoy a woman or two. The theory is that men got together and agreed to each having his own woman, and that no other man, under threat of penalties, was to approach her. Thus the men were freed to concentrate on the hunt. Another example of the biological roots of marriage: man brings home the meat while the woman cooks it, makes the clothes, tends the children, and takes care of the adjacent garden plot.

Government is an example of another social institution with a biological basis. If men were filled with the milk of human kindness and only wanted to follow the golden rule, then governments would not be necessary. However, in reality, man is dominated by the Expanding Programs of his Biologically Programmed Computer. He wants to exploit his fellow man, and to use the products of his fellow man's labor for his own needs. Mankind wants power in the form of money and in the form of control.

Following the death of Senator Kennedy, President Johnson appointed a committee to look into the cause of violence in America. He gave them a list of social issues to be investigated, but not one word was mentioned about the biological cause of violence. How many of the members of the committee were biologists or biochemists? This is only another example of man's reactionary, outdated, unscientific approach to the problems which beset him.

Science has enabled man to live in cities and science has robbed man of his most powerful programmers. It is only fair that science now should solve the problems which it helped create. But human nature, being what it is, will probably not allow science to attack mankind's problems until his social life becomes a shambles. It is only hoped that man can survive.

Man loves his theories and follows them to the bitter end. He is still following the theory that social ills can be cured through alteration in social structure. He still acts on the outmoded theory that man is the center of the universe and, therefore, above biological forces. Man enjoys dressing in well pressed clothes, jetting through the stratosphere faster than the speed of sound, and making fine speeches on television. Man is inclined to forget that he, just as the hyena or a chimpanzee, would die if he did not eat, breathe, and drink water. Woman gives birth to a child who will someday reach old age, die, and disintegrate.

A quote from Robert Ardrey's open-minded book, *The Territorial Imperative*, may help orient the reader to a biological approach to social problems:

> If you are an adolescent chacma baboon of overly bellicose nature and your aggression leads you to pick quarrels again and again with fellow members of your troop, then the chances are that someday you will get hurt. And you will not be able to keep up with your troop as it moves about your range seeking food. And you will fall behind and a leopard will eat you. Your troop will be better for it, since baboons simply cannot survive without their highly organized cooperative societies. This capacity to form disciplined societies is the baboon's most valuable genetic endowment. You were a variant, but happily you leave no offspring since the leopard has eaten you.

Here we see an example of nature cleaning up the genetic pool of a society by eliminating undesirable genes. We humans, when we get into a street fight and are taken to a hospital, are given medical help and are cared for until we recover. The excessively aggressive human is thus not eliminated by nature. His genes remain to plague society.

Since the bearers of man's inappropriate traits (BPC) tend not to be weeded out by nature*, it might be well for man to sit down and use the tool which is both his blessing and, more and more, his curse—the mind. The mind of man, if it were used logically, tells one that man must logically decide which traits (BPC) are valuable to society, which help mankind survive, and which traits are unfavorable.

Since man does not allow his bearers of inappropriate traits to be eaten by leopards, he must devise other means to gradually eliminate them, or else use chemical means to control the behavior which results from socially damaging traits. As Paddock and Paddock pointed out, mankind is over-populating the earth. His reproduction must be sharply curtailed if he is to survive. Logically the limitation upon reproduction should start with the members of society who harbor a high percentage of the least favorable traits.

At this point of the discussion you may shout "genocide," "Hitlerism," "Brave New World," and in general pull out dragoons and shoot off fire-

---

* This is largely because of man's humanistic philosophy which tries to deny his biological roots and pretend that men, like little girls, are made of sugar and spice and everything nice, and that all everyone needs is more love, freedom, and charity, to eliminate all man's anger and murderous inclinations.

crackers. Very well, but rather than being emotional about it, let us return to the realm of the mind.

First, remember we are discussing the survival of the human species. Survival in itself is no mean undertaking in the course of evolution. One fact is certain—it is very possible for a species to perish because it is unable to adapt to changing environmental conditions.

The very human traits (Expanding Programs of the Biologically Programmed Computer) which saved mankind from the sabertoothed tiger and the Ice Ages, and helped him drag home enough meat for the cave, are now a threat to mankind. The environment of the Europe of 50,000 years ago was quite different from the environment of New York City's East 60's during the second half of the 20th century. Each of these environments requires a different set of traits (Biologically Programmed Computer).

As pointed out before, man was bred as a killer (strong killing programs in his Expanding Programs of his Biologically Programmed Computer). This killing trait was quite an advantage in the days of the fang, but in the era of atomic weaponry, it is the great threat to the survival of the species.

It would seem logical that mankind's Expanding Programs must be modified if he is to survive his technology. Man must be biologically changed. This can be done by either changing his genetic makeup, by selective breeding, or by a chemical reduction of the forces of his Expanding Drives.

By this point, you may have waxed emotional again. In your mind you may have science fiction pictures of a world of humanoid robots. Dismiss these images. In place of these weird scientific fictions, picture the best adjusted, happiest, easiest going man you know, one who is pleasant, inoffensive, and slow to fight.

Frank McGee of the Today's Show is well known by many readers. From watching his program we have a certain knowledge about him, if not the real man, then at least about the image he projects on television. It is this image (rather than the real man, which may or may not be the same) which we are discussing. He appears to be a basically happy man who is not particularly aggressive or quick to fight. Contrast him with Jack Paar who was always publicly at war with someone.

How would Frank McGee have fared had he lived 50,000 years ago? Probably he would not have been rough enough (had strong enough Killing Programs in the Expanding Programs of his Biologically Programmed Computer) to have eaten very well. But if all the men in the world today had Biologically Programmed Computers like Frank McGee, think how much more peaceful the world would be. If the leaders of Israel and of Egypt were men like Frank McGee, wouldn't they somehow work out their differences at the negotiating table? Would weaponry be usurping eighty billions of dollars of the national budget if the world were populated by Frank McGees?

People are loath to give up their rights of reproduction, partly because reproduction is a part of their Expanding Programs. To be a member of a large family is to have more power. To have children is amusing, a change of pace, a possible security for old age. Besides, married people are expected to bear children, otherwise they are not "normal." Everyone who has had children knows, however, that they are a mixed blessing and a generally overrated pleasure. Could many people give up the pleasure of bearing children for the greater good of humanity? Could people make this noble sacrifice knowing that they are making a significant contribution to the survival of humanity?

Perhaps these people who are selected not to reproduce (a license is required for marriage, a second license could be issued for the right to reproduce) could be given a significant title in recognition of their noble sacrifice for the human species. The government could well afford to reward them annually at a handsome rate. With such a program perhaps the species could be saved and the nonreproducers could feel well rewarded for their sacrifices for the common good.

Other biological approaches could be used. The genetic formations of man could be altered through a chemical alteration of the DNA (deoxyribonucleic acid). This is the genetic material which determines both the physical and chemical makeup of each cell in the body. Hence DNA controls that part of behavior which stems from the Biologically Programmed Computer. By altering the DNA it should be possible to biologically alter behavioral traits and thus turn man into a being with milder BPC Expanding Programs, with increased tractability and with the decreased killing programs which he has inappropriately inherited from the days when he depended upon hunting for survival. If these programs are modified, then man's anger would automatically be reduced in degree. The chemist has transferred DNA from one bacteria to another and in so doing altered forever the host's characteristics, but this operation has not yet been performed on man. In another twenty to fifty years alteration in man's BPC by altering his DNA may well be possible.

Other biological solutions could be found for solving mankind's social and psychological problems, but some of them would probably be too foreign to man's basic orientation to be acceptable to him. For example, males could be eliminated as effective members of society. The ants have solved their social problems in this manner and have survived and maintained great social stability for more than fifty million years.

A glance at history will confirm the fact that the inheritance of many strong programs in the BPC (Expanding Programs, Behavioral Programs such as tractability, energy level, killing) are sex linked. The human male, not the female, has been bred for two million years to fulfill the role of killer, protector, meat gatherer, inventor. The male, and not the female, has Expanding Programs which force him to tear away at social institutions, at Skinner boxes.

Do we have a female Alexander the Great? Napoleon?, Hitler?, Copernicus?, Marx?, Freud?, Einstein? Was it a male or a female who slayed Christ, Caesar, Charles I, Louis XVI, Lincoln, Archduke Ferdinand, Kennedy, King? Is it the male or the female who fights the wars, builds atomic weapons, ignites the rockets? Clearly man is the creature who causes most of the turmoil among Homo sapiens. Will the reader grant that man is chemically, biologically (BPC) different from woman and that no number of social programs, education, minimum wages will give man the characteristics of a woman?

It might be possible to allow females a sexual (if not the satisfaction of a more complex male-female social relationship) relationship by having all males operated upon at birth. A small destruction of the male brain could take away most of the anti-social aspects of his BPC and still leave him free to perform sexually. These methods have obvious disadvantages for all of us. The solutions discussed were only used to illustrate a biological possibility.

Today mankind has already begun attacking social problems with biological tools. We see prisoners, members of reformatory schools, and dischargees from psychiatric hospitals receiving tranquilizers (psychochemistry) for an indefinite period of time. Their aggressive, dissocial behavior is successfully treated as a biochemical disorder and, like the diabetic, these persons are given the chemical needed to keep them in social equilibrium.

One of the disadvantages of using chemical means for the reduction of aggressions and other antisocial behavior is that members of society who harbor these undesirable genes tend to pass on their genes in ever greater numbers. Evidence clearly shows that the chances of offspring developing schizophrenia vary from 10% when one parent is schizophrenic to 50% when both parents are so affected.

As Rainer of Columbia University pointed out in his article in Freedman's *Comprehensive Textbook of Psychiatry*, at the turn of the century the reproductive rate for schizophrenics was about half that of the general population. Today, with shorter hospitalizations due to psychochemotherapy, the schizophrenic's rate of reproduction is almost equal to that of the general population.

Should, through selective reproduction or through genetic engineering, schizophrenia be eliminated from the human species? This is a difficult question to answer. Certainly persons suffering from schizophrenia have and do contribute much to the human condition. In centuries past he most certainly, in the aggressive, borderline form, did much to help the survival of the tribe. He must have been first in war and first in exploration and first in furnishing the drive needed to clear the forests.

And, because of their perceptual alterations, persons suffering from the schizophrenia syndrome see the world, the relationships in the world, in a different light, and hence are more likely to be inventive. The man who invented the wheel may well have been suffering from schizophrenia. Of course, whether the world is better off having the wheel is a moot question which still has not yet been settled.

In the arts the schizophrenic reigns supreme. Because he sees the world in a different way and transmits this vision through his art for the rest of mankind, his productions are refreshing. The novels of Hemingway and the paintings of Cézanne give man a new breath of air and help him bear his boredom. Whether it is fair to ask men to live with the emotional pain with which Hemingway and Cézanne lived, is another question which must someday be answered.

As Hoffer and Osmond pointed out, the recovered schizophrenic has a biological and psychological toughness which is hardly matched by any other members of society. He not only withstands such biological trauma as blood loss, for example, better than his neighbor, but can often endure great emotional hardship. Will these traits someday be of value to humanity when jetting through space to occupy a distant galaxy? Who can say for certain?

In the end it would seem to this author that the real question is not whether a man does or does not suffer from schizophrenia, but rather what is his level of anger and destructiveness. Some so-called normal people are destructive and some are not. Some people suffering from schizophrenia are destructive, and some are not. Destruction in any form is a threat to all humanity. There is no question but that we could do without the Hitlers. The Hemingways are, basically, a problem only to themselves.

Man is a clever animal. He produces sugar to decay his teeth and then produces dentists to fill the cavities. He produces tobacco to give him cancer and then invents X-rays to diagnose the disease and educates surgeons to eradicate it.

Perhaps mankind will continue to produce socially difficult people in ever larger waves and invent clever psychochemistry to make social living possible for them. Perhaps, like fluorides, psychochemicals will one day be added to the drinking water. It is estimated today in this country, between 25 to 50% of the population takes psychotrophic chemicals. The figure would be higher if people who used alcohol, tobacco, and patent psychotrophic chemicals were added to the number. In summary it may be said that man's anger, as well as the other antisocial aspects of his personality, is solidly based upon his biological makeup, his BPC.

No matter how many billions of dollars are spent in attempting to ease man's lot, to give him more food and better housing, it will not erase his anger or do away with his killing programs. Like a child given a new toy, man puts what he has in his pocket, turns to look for something else and is angry if he does not forever get more: more food, more housing, more entertainment, more toys, more power, more opportunity to kill, for this is man's biological inheritance. Only by changing his biological makeup can man be changed.

What method can we find to bring about the alteration? The author sincerely hopes better methods than eliminating the male can be found, but he believes the solutions to our social problems and to our problem of survival must be biological.

New York
August, 1971.

References

Adler, A. *The science of living.* New York: Greenberg, 1929.

Adler, I. *Thinking machines.* New York: John Day, 1961.

Agency for International Development, Statistics and Reports Division. *Selected economic data for the less developed countries.* June, 1965.

Alexander, F. G., & Selesnick, S. T. *The history of psychiatry.* New York: Harper & Row, 1966.

Axelrod, J. Control of catecholamine and indoleamine metabolism by sympathetic nerves. *Mechanisms of release of biogenic amines.* New York: Pergamon, 1966.

Barnett, S. A. Behavior components in the feeding of wild and laboratory rats. *Behaviour* IX, 1956, 24–43.

Bender, L. Childhood schizophrenia. *International Journal of Psychiatry*, March, 1968.

Berlin, I. *Karl Marx.* London: Oxford University Press, 1963.

Berman, L. *The religion celled behaviorism.* New York: Boni & Liverright, 1927.

Bischof, L. J. *Interpreting personality theories.* New York: Harper & Row, 1964.

Blackham, H. J. *Six Existentialist Thinkers.* London: Routledge and Kegan Paul, 1952.

Boulding, K. E. *The image.* Ann Arbor, Mich.: University of Michigan Press, 1956.

Brown, L. R. Address before the Pacific Northwest Farm Forum, Spokane, Washington, Feb. 8, 1966.

Cherry, C. *On human communication.* Cambridge: M.I.T. Press, 1966.

Cook, L., & Kelleher, R. T. Effects of drugs on behavior. *Annual Review of Pharmacology*, 1963, **3**, 205–222.

Cooper, J. E. A study of behavior therapy in thirty psychiatric patients. *Lancet*, 1963, **1**, 411.

Croissant, J. *Aristole et les mysteres.* Liége: Faculte de Philosophie et Lettres, 1932.

Cruickshank, W. M. *The brain injured child in home, school, and community.* Syracuse: Syracuse University Press, 1967.

Darlington, C. D. *The evolution of man and society.* London: Allen and Unwin, 1969.

Davydov, Y. Knight of the revolution. *Soviet Life*, 1967 (No. 3), 126. Washington, D.C. The Embassy of the Union of Soviet Socialist Republics.

Diebold, J. *Automation.* Princeton: Van Nostrand, 1952.

Eysenck, H. J. The effects of psychotherapy—An evaluation. *Journal of Consulting Psychology*, 1952, **16**, 319–23.

Ferster, C. B., & Skinner, B. F. *Schedules of reinforcement.* New York: Appleton-Century-Crofts, 1957.

Flores, I. *Computer programming.* New York: Prentice-Hall, 1966.

Ford, C. E., & Hamerston, J. L. The chromosomes of man. *Nature*, 1956, **178**, 1020.

Ford, D. H., & Urban, H. B. *Systems of psychotherapy.* New York: Wiley, 1963.

Fox, M. W. *Canine behavior.* Springfield, Ill.: Charles C. Thomas, 1965.

Freed, H. *The chemistry and therapy of behavior disorders in children.* Springfield, Ill.: Charles C. Thomas, 1962.

Freedman, A. M., & Kaplan, H. I. *Comprehensive textbook of psychiatry.* Baltimore: Williams & Wilkins, 1967.

Freud, S. *Complete psychological works of Sigmund Freud* (Trans. and Ed. by J. Strachey). London: Hogarth Press, and Institute of Psychoanalysis, 1953.

Freud, S. From L. C. Kolb, *Noyes' modern clinical psychiatry.* Philadelphia: W. B. Saunders, 1968, p. 574.

Genetics of chromosomes and crime. *Time,* May 3, 1968, p. 41.

Gesell, A., & Amatruda, C. S. *Development diagnosis: Normal and abnormal development.* New York: Paul B. Hoeber, 1947.

Ginsberg, B. E. Genetics as a tool in the study of behavior. *Perspectives in Biology and Medicine,* (1958) Vol. 1, pp. 397–424.

Gordon, H. L. *The new chemotherapy of mental illness.* New York: Philosophical Library, 1958.

Gordon, P. Diphenylhydrantoin and procainamide normalization of suboptimal learning behavior. In J. Wortis (Ed.), *Recent advances in biological psychiatry,* Vol. IX. New York: Plenum Press, 1967.

Granik, D. *The red executive.* London: Macmillan, 1960.

Heath, R. G. A biochemical hypotheses on the etiology of schizophrenia. In D. O. Jackson (Ed.), *The etiology of schizophrenia.* New York: Basic Books, 1960. p. 146.

Hirsch, J. Behavior genetics and individuality understood. *Science,* 1963, **142,** 1436–1442.

Hoffer, A. *Niacin therapy in psychiatry.* Springfield, Ill.: Charles C. Thomas, 1962.

Hoffer, A., & Osmond, H. *How to live with schizophrenia.* New York: University Books, 1966.

Holland, J. G., & Skinner, B. T. *The analysis of behavior.* New York: McGraw-Hill, 1961.

Honig, W. K. (Ed.) *Operant behavior, areas of research and application.* New York: Appleton-Century-Crofts, 1966.

Jones, E. *The life and works of Sigmund Freud.* New York: Basic Books, 1953.

Jung, C. G. *Psychological types.* New York: Harcourt, Brace & World, 1923.

Jung, C. G. *The collected works* (Ed. by H. Read.). New York: Pantheon, 1960.

Kallmann, Franz J. The genetics of mental illness, In S. Arieti (Ed.), *American handbook of psychiatry.* New York: Basic Books, 1959. pp. 175–196.

Kallmann, Franz J. The Genetic Theory of Schizophrenia, *American Journal of Psychiatry,* 1946, **103,** 309–22.

Kanner, L. *Child psychiatry.* Springfield, Ill.: Charles C. Thomas, 1962.

Kety, S. Biochemical theories of schizophrenia, *International Journal of Psychiatry,* 1965. **1,** 409–47.

Kimble, G. A., & Garmezy, N. *Principles of general psychology.* New York: Ronald Press, 1963.

Kline, N. S., & Lehmann, H. E. *Psychopharmacology.* Boston: Little, Brown and Company, 1965.

Kolb, L. C. *Noyes' modern clinical psychiatry.* Philadelphia: W. B. Saunders, 1968.

Kraepelin, E. *Psychiatrie, ein Lehrbuch für Studierende und Arzte,* ed. 5, Barth, Leipzig, 1896.

Krech, D., & Crutchfield, R. S. *Elements of psychology.* New York: Alfred A. Knopf, 1962.

Kringlen, E. *Heredity and environment in the functional psychoses.* Universitetsforlaget, Oslo (William Heinemann Medical Books, London), 1967.

Laurie, E. J. *Computers and computer languages.* Cincinnati: Southwestern Publishing Company, 1966.

Lindsey, G., & Hall, C. S. *Theories of personality: Primary sources and research.* New York: Wiley, 1965.

Mark, V. H. The neurology of behavior: Its application to human violence. *Medical Opinion & Review,* April, 1968, **4,** 4.

Masserman, J. H. *The practice of dynamic psychiatry.* Philadelphia: W. B. Saunders, 1955.

May, R., Angel E., & Ellenberger, H. F. (Eds.) *Existence: A new dimension in psychiatry and psychology.* New York: Basic Books, 1958.

Meier, C. *Antike Inkubation und Modern Psychotherapie.* Zurich: Rascher, 1949.

Miller, W. J., Roberts, H. L., & Shulman, M. D. *The meaning of communism.* Morristown: Silver Burdett Company, 1963.

Moody, P. A. *Genetics of man.* New York: W. W. Norton, 1967.

Morris, D. *The naked ape.* New York: McGraw-Hill, 1967.

Newbold, H. L. 1/3 *of an inch of french bread.* New York: Crowell, 1961.

Newbold, H. L., & Steed, W. D. The use of chlorpromazine in psychotherapy. In H. L. Gordon (Ed.), *The new chemotherapy in mental illness,* New York: Philosophical Library, 1958. p. 310.

O'Neil, C. F., & Travisono, A. D. *Correctional chemotherapy.* Eldora, Iowa State Training School for Boys, 1968.

Osborn, F. *The future of human heredity.* New York: Weybright and Talley, 1968.

Pauling, L. Orthomolecular psychiatry. *Science,* 1968, **160,** 265.

Peterson, D. R., & London, P. A. A role for cognition in the behavioral treatment of child's elimination disturbance. In L. P. Ullmann and L. Krasner (Eds.), *Case studies in behavior modification.* New York: Holt, Rinehart & Winston, 1965.

Pfaffenberger, C. J. *The new knowledge of dog behavior.* New York: Howell Book House, 1963.

Pfeiffer, E. *Disordered behavior.* New York: Oxford University Press, 1968.

Phillips, E. L., & Wiener, D. N. *Short-term psychotherapy and structured behavior change.* New York: McGraw-Hill, 1966.

Pines, M. *New York Times Magazine,* July 6, 1969.

Polatin, P. *A guide to treatment in psychiatry.* Philadelphia: J. B. Lippincott.

Population Bulletin of the United Nations, No. 6 (1962).

Population Reference Bureau, Washington, D. C. *World Population Data Sheet,* December, 1965.

Porter, L. H. The genetics of drug susceptibility. *Dis. Nerv. System,* 1966, **27,** 25–36.

Rogers, C. R. *Counseling and psychotherapy.* Boston: Houghton Mifflin, 1942.

Rostand, J. *Can man be modified?* New York: Basic Books, 1959.

Sargent, W., & Slater, E. *An introduction to physical methods of treatment in psychiatry.* Baltimore: Williams and Wilkins, 1964.

Schildkraut, J. J. The catecholamine hypothesis of affective disorders: A review of supporting evidence. *American Journal of Psychiatry,* 1965, **122,** 509–522.

Science News, Vol. 93, 20 April, 1968.

Scott, J. P. *Aggression.* Chicago: University of Chicago Press, 1958.

Scott, J. P., & Fuller, J. L. *Genetics and the social behavior of the dog.* Chicago: University of Chicago Press, 1965.

Scott, T. G. *Computer programming techniques.* New York: Doubleday & Company, 1964.

Shields, J. *Monozygotic twins.* New York: Oxford University Press, 1962.

Shirley, H. F. *Pediatric psychiatry.* Cambridge: Harvard University Press, 1963.

Sidman, M. Behavioral pharmacology. *Psychopharmacol.,* 1959, **1,** 179.

Skinner, B. F. Drive and reflex strength. *J. Gen. Psychol.,* 1932, **6,** 38–48.

Skinner, B. F. Two types of conditioned reflex: A reply to Konorski and Miller. *J. Gen. Psychol.,* 1937, **16,** 272–279.

Skinner, B. F. Are theories of learning necessary? *Psychol. Rev.,* 1950, **57,** 193–216.

Skinner, B. F. *Verbal behavior.* New York: Appleton-Century-Crofts, 1957.

Skinner, B. F. *Cumulative record.* New York: Appleton-Century-Crofts, 1961.

Skinner, B. F. Behavorism at fifty. *Science,* 1963, **140,** 951–958.

Skinner, B. F. *The behavior of organisms.* New York: Appleton-Century-Crofts, 1968.

Spencer, L. L. *The use of psychiatric medication at the Iowa training school for boys.* Eldora, Iowa State Training School for Boys, 1967.

Stevenson, Ian. The challenge of results in psychotherapy, *American Journal of Psychiatry,* 1959, **116,** 120–23.

Toman, J. E. P. Neuropharmacology of diphanylhydration, *International Journal of Neuropsychiatry*, Vol. 3, Supplement 2, (December 1967).

Ware, Thomas. Testimony before the Senate Subcommittee on Economic and Social Policy of the Foreign Relations Committee, June 29, 1965.

Watson, E. H., & Lowrey, G. H. *Growth and development of children*. Chicago: Year Book Medical Publishers, 1967.

Watson, J. B. *Behaviorism*. Chicago: University of Chicago Press, 1924.

Watson, R. L. *The great psychologists from Aristotle to Freud*. Philadelphia: J. B. Lippincott, 1963.

Wepman, J. M., & Heine, R. W. *Concepts of personality*. Chicago: Aldine, 1963.

Whitney, T. P. *Russia in my life*. London: Harrap, 1963.

Wiener, N. *Cybernetics*. New York: Wiley, 1948.

Wiener, N. *The human use of human beings*. Boston: Houghton Mifflin, 1950.

Williams, D. The significance of an abnormal electroencephalogram. *Journal of Neurology and Psychiatry*, 1941, **4**, 267.

Wilson, I. G., & Wilson, M. E. *Information, computers, and design systems*. New York: Wiley, 1967.

Wolpe, J. *Psychotherapy by reciprocal inhibition*. Palo Alto: Stanford University, 1963.

Woodworth, R. S., & Sheehan, M. R. *Contemporary schools of psychology*. New York: Ronald Press, 1964.

Yates, A. J. *Behavior therapy*, New York: Wiley, 1970.

Zilbourg, G. *A history of medical psychology*. New York: W. W. Norton, 1941.